The SWORD of Leadership

The SWORD of Leadership

Become the Leader You Are Meant to Be

Onward Miles Christianus!

—Thom Owens

Dr. Thom Owens

ISBN-13: 9781793430939
Imprint: Independently published by Strategic Influence Alternatives, LLC

Internal Design and Illustrations by the Author
Cover design: Brandy Powell

Dedication

I would like to dedicate this book to the many leaders, too many to mention, who have refined my understanding of leadership and helped me to consistently model the type of leadership this book seeks to capture, especially Jesus, the ultimate example of the leader we should all aspire to be.

Acknowledgments

Proverbs 15:22 (NIV) tells us, "Plans fail for lack of counsel, but with many advisers they succeed." Specifically, I would like to thank all of those who have counselled, advised and encouraged me to write this book: Dr. Kathleen Patterson who planted the seed when I began to describe the initial concepts of the model; Dr. Joseph Umidi, who inspired me to put this material together into a book; Dr. Joseph Bucci, who provided valuable feedback to make this book better; Dr. Bob Grymes, Keith Powell, Brandy Powell, Ed Carr, Jeff Ganthner, Joseph Perry, Elaine Lankford, Bishop Dr. Perry Austin, Pastor Joel Walker, Mike Klausmeier, Tom Noon, Pastor Paul Martin, Dr. Prentis McGoldrick, Travis Hall and Clay Robertson who all read the early manuscripts and provided feedback and encouragement; Dr. David Abbott for the divine inspiration for the name of the model; Brandy Powell for her design of the book cover, Erlene Weldon, my editor, who helped me communicate these ideas more effectively, and all the other people in my life who have offered encouragement and inspiration along the way.

Most importantly I want to thank my wife, Tonya and my girls, Rachel, Madison, Lindsey and Lauren for supporting me through the process and encouraging me on to completion.

Praise for The SWORD of Leadership

"You might wonder if we really need another book on leadership. I would suggest in the affirmative, yes, we do! We need another book on leadership because the world is desperate for leaders of conviction and courage, and the current crop of leadership books are proving inadequate to accomplish this task. Dr. Owens has articulated his great vision of stable and mature leadership, with images of a solid structure that defines the type of person who will remain true to their leadership values no matter the obstacles. The avatars of the knights that represent the qualities of leadership are vivid and memorable. The integration and application of scripture is well-thought-out and helps the reader to know how to apply the lesson learned. Overall, an enjoyable and challenging read."
Dr. Joseph J. Bucci, Associate Professor and Department Chair Business, Leadership and Management Department, College of Arts and Sciences, Regent University

"Thom delivers as a leader who has gone through and lives the struggle of finding peace in life. If you have time to read only one chapter, read Chapter 2 - The Citadel of Peace - it will change how you see God and his purpose for your life."
Jeffrey Ganthner, AIA, Vice President, Burns & McDonnell and Founder, leadershiphunt.com

"In *The SWORD of Leadership*, Dr. Thom Owens demonstrates a masterful understanding of true Christian Leadership and provides the biblical infrastructure necessary for believers to live out their purpose."
Joseph Perry, Pastor, Remnant Ministries; Author, *The Go Book: Foundations*

"If you are a leader who wants to get better, you need to invest in yourself and get this book."
Keith Powell, Principal, Apex Financial Consulting

"Through the biblical and historical approach in this model, the complexity of leadership is broken down in an easy to understand approach and implementation made easy with small building blocks in each chapter. Your time will be well spent no matter your leadership background to pick up *The SWORD of Leadership*."
Ed Carr, Founder, Edward Carr & Associates

"True Christ-centered leadership often eludes us. The integration of our faith into areas such as the marketplace, where many of us lead, has not been written about enough or written with the boldness that we as Christians are called to. In *The SWORD of Leadership,* Dr. Owens presents with precision the key disciplines we as Christian

leaders should strive to possess and build upon as we grow in our leadership abilities. Most importantly, he has rightly pointed back to the only foundation in which anything in our lives should be built upon - Jesus Christ. The path to improvement is paved with continual assessment of where we currently stand. By using the framework provided within this book, Christian leaders will be able to pinpoint their current strengths and weaknesses in five specific areas, and therefore, bolster their God-given leadership abilities by seeking God's best in those areas of need."
Elaine A. Lankford, Founder, Speaker, and Leadership Coach, Transforming Love Ministries; Author, *Love Echoed Back: I Cried Out, He Answered*

"Thom Owens did a wonderful job of giving a full understanding of what it is to be a Christian Leader. In a world that many will see many versions of leadership. Thom brings clarity to finding your true purpose by giving the tools needed to succeed!"
Bishop Dr. Perry L. Austin, Founder, Leverage Academy of Business and Leadership

"I have known Dr. Thom Owens for over 30 years and have watched him grow and develop in his leadership skills to become one of America's top authorities in Leadership Development. And I am not surprised. As a teenager in his church youth group, Thom was respected and followed by others because of his early leadership skills. Through the years Thom has lived out all that he teaches. His new book, *The SWORD of Leadership*, is well-illustrated with a clear picture of the desired outcome (a Paladin). Thom shows you the finished product and how to achieve it with a step-by-step approach. If you want God to give you the plans He has for you, there must be large-capacity growth in your life to handle it! I highly recommend this book to all who want to receive God's plan and become the leader they desire and thrive in the Citadel of Peace."
Joel R. Walker, Pastor, Teacher, Certified Chaplain with Corporate Chaplains of America

"The book's approach to the subject with its avatar-stories and biblical-based examples should appeal to all, Christian and non-Christian, alike. *The SWORD of Leadership* should enhance a leader's ability to lead by example and serve others by employing caring, honesty, and integrity – characteristics sorely needed in todays' public and corporate sectors.

"Exercising leadership in accord with the Biblical principles presented in the book cannot help but result in success in business and in relationships. I truly believe that reading *The SWORD of Leadership* and applying its values will not only make one a better, more effective leader, it could well change one's life."
Dr. Bob Grymes, Retired Educator

"Leadership, in today's age and culture, is not something that we are taught from childhood. It's something that, as adults, we seek to learn. I appreciate Thom's heart for the cultivating of leadership in life and in business. He speaks the truth plainly and

frankly as he shares the implications of good leadership vs. the lack of leadership. Although his desire is to shore up men as leaders in our society and workplace, he also recognizes and highlights the leadership role and ability of women in his profiling of Deborah. It really doesn't matter your job, calling, or stage in life, this book is full of wisdom based on Biblical principles that apply to everyone."
Brandy Powell, Speaker and Author, *Bent Not Broken: Facing Crisis and Keeping the Faith* and *Lessons from My Closet: Finding Your Foundation in Faith & Life*

"Thom Owens has combined his deep faith, his advanced education, and his valuable Army experience into a unique, useful and practical book that serves as a roadmap to Christian maturity. I highly recommend this book to everyone who is seeking a fresh approach to the attainment of the next level of Christian leadership."
Mike Klausmeier, Founder, Redox Resource Engineering, Author, *Corporation Reformation*

"I am an avid reader on leadership, business, brain science and even physics because they all tend to intersect when they interact with PEOPLE. But the main intersection I am interested in is how the Bible intersects with all the current philosophies and trends about how organizations survive and scale.

"At their core, every organization is also about PEOPLE. How God uniquely and wonderfully made each one of us then sent us each on a Journey to find and follow Him. Some find Him and some do not, but the basic laws of the universe were set in place by God because He has a plan, and His plan involves us.

"I have known Dr. Thom Owens for several years and I know him to have a passion for both leadership and God. In my book, that is a great combo! I have also seen Thom in action, leading our local Christian Business Coalition, so know him to be a committed, trustworthy, dedicated leader. He is a man you want to learn leadership principles from!

"Thom built a career as a military officer learning leadership in the trenches, then broadened his understanding of leadership in the classroom getting a doctorate in Leadership from perhaps the top Christian University on the subject.

"In *The SWORD of Leadership,* Thom melds all this with one important addition, the leading of the Holy Spirit.

"Perhaps God's plan for you is organizational leadership, or even leadership in your family and other spheres of your life. Regardless of the target, the 'SWORD of Leadership' will give you a great leg up on achieving your calling!"
Thomas Noon, Founder, C-Level Services and Catalyst Cohorts.

"The SWORD of Leadership is a clear and fresh biblical perspective on the core issue of leadership - that great leaders are godly people. The analogies of "the Citadel of

Peace" and "the Paladin" create a concise concept that develop "a life infrastructure" to support your "God-sized dream" which is both portable and practical. Thom offers us wisdom from his personal experiences and time in scripture with the Lord that he shares in a creative and imaginative way so that we can personally identify with our need to overcome fear and presuppositions so that we can become Paladins for Christ. Thom's desire is that everyone responds to the call of the Paladin and realizes that: "To participate in God's plan is to participate in the ultimate organizational change initiative, the redemption of creation by advancing the banner of Christ." Dr. Owens communicates a concept that will challenge your thoughts and goals and he leaves you with tools to rise to this challenge for the glory of God. This is an important read for any follower of Jesus that desires to honor Christ."
Paul Martin, Senior Pastor, Fairview Baptist Church

"Fantastic read for those looking to find their "WHY." The principles in this book are focused on helping people to get engaged in their purpose. Each of us possesses leadership qualities. This book helps you define and nurture those principles. I highly recommend reading it."
Clay Robertson, Principal, WBR Insurance

"I have read many books on leadership. Most of them rearrange the chapters but say the same things. Dr. Thom Owens writes about leadership as a change of character rather than merely focusing on results. Results are always important but who the leader is determines whether the leadership should be reproduced. That is the key to long-term growth in an organization. Passing the skills along to others is more than teaching them what to do. It is leading them to become a leader that is respected and emulated by the people in the organization. This is the essence of *The SWORD of Leadership*. Reading the book won't change you. Becoming what the book espouses will. This book should be read by every leader and kept on his or her shelf for reference."
Dr. Prentis McGoldrick, Senior Pastor, Thalia Lynn Baptist Church

"What Thom has done in *The Sword of Leadership* is provide leaders with a tool with a perfect blend of Biblical and Leadership principles. This book will not only enable leaders to find who they are called to be as a leader but also do the same with their teams."
Travis Hall, Executive Director, Youth Challenge of Hampton Roads

Free Bonus Gift

One of the challenges that create limiting beliefs for many Christian leaders is the lack of awareness of their purpose. Because I want you to get the most out of this book, I am offering you access to some resources that will help you in this area.

Go to www.swordofleadership.com and there you will find a video workshop with a workbook for digging deeper into your purpose.

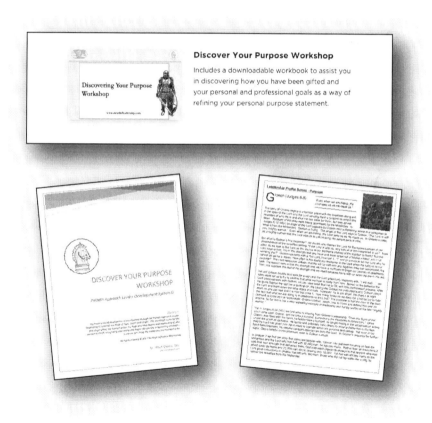

Forward

In Medieval Europe the Gospel was visually preached annually as traveling carts set up in towns to reenact the life and times of Jesus and the disciples. Before any research on right brain/left brain there was a deep intuition that seeing, and hearing were integral for receiving. Moses knew it at the burning bush, and the Emmaus Road disciples knew it when the resurrected Christ broke bread in their sight.

When the "seer" Habakkuk lost his perspective on how to see the hand of God in a godless generation, he knew what the next step had to be.

> *I will take my stand at my watchpost*
> *and station myself on the tower,*
> *and look out to see what he will say to me,*
> *and what I will answer concerning my complaint.*
> Habakkuk 2:1 (ESV)

The SWORD of Leadership is for the atrophied seer in all of us. It is an answer to the fireworks that have replaced our burning bushes, the Twinkies that have substituted for our Emmaus Road broken bread, the cartoon super-heroes that have crowded out our watchtower anticipations. In this creative metaphor of formations, discipleship, and leadership development, Dr. Thom has made the complicated simple and the foundational advanced.

I have hope that boomers can connect to millennials and "z" generation with the creative power of this read. It offers common word pictures that gives us a common kingdom language; helping us all to stand on a common ground together. The end result is the hope of an uncommon intergenerational honoring of the gospel embraced by all generations.

I want to see this book become a family board game, a discipleship tool at churches, a leadership credential in schools. Most of all I want to see it reignite your passion to be the man and woman of God that is purposed in the heart of the Author and Finisher of our faith. And that would make my friend and colleague, Dr. Thom, the leader he is meant to be.

Dr. Joseph Umidi
EVP Regent University
Founder, Lifeforming Institute

Preface

This book is a result of my personal development journey as a leader. I am a product of one of the world's best leadership laboratories, the US Army. I spent over 24 years developing and refining my skills and abilities as a leader of Soldiers, training for and executing complex missions, leading others in challenging and demanding environments all around the globe. When I retired, I transferred those skills, abilities and experiences into the corporate world and have held executive positions in both for profit and non-profit entities, but I could not initially find my niche.

During that transition period while I was in search of my purpose, I decided to pursue my doctorate in Strategic Leadership and it was then that the model in this book was developed. I was holding on to Jeremiah 29:11 knowing that God has a plan for me to prosper me and not harm me, to give me a hope and a future, but I got a little impatient with God's timing. So, one day in desperation I asked the question, "When?" Don't ever ask God a question unless you are ready for the answer. The answer I got was very simple, yet profound.

"When you are ready to handle the God-sized purpose I have for you."

The reality was that I did not have the life infrastructure in place to handle that God-sized purpose. God revealed that the purpose He has for me would crush me if

He gave it to me in my then present state and that He loved me too much to do that to me. So instead of asking "when," I started asking for "how" and "what." How do I develop the life infrastructure to be the leader God intends for me to be? What does that look like? That journey of discovery resulted in the model at the heart of this book, the Citadel of Peace©, and the system that model represents, the Paladin Approach Leader Development System©. This system and the model within it are not intended to be the next leadership fad. They are intended to be something that anyone can order their life around to keep them focused on being the best version of themselves that they can be.

My motivation for writing this book is to share my model and the insights I gained while developing it so that I might spare you some of the frustrations I experienced while I figured this out. Through this journey of personal development, I have identified the essential elements of what it means to develop as a leader in pursuit of my God-sized purpose. My hope is to be your guide on your personal development journey into the leader that God intends for you to be.

If you are thinking, that is all well and good, but I don't necessarily consider myself a leader let me just stop you right there and assure you that being a leader is not about titles or positions in large corporations. The number one person you must learn to lead well is yourself. This is the first level (and frankly the hardest sometimes) of leadership and the main focus of this book. Once you learn to lead yourself well, it gets easier to lead others well. I'm looking forward to accompanying you on your journey of development as a leader and I hope that you find value in the pages of this book.

The format for this book is one that not only describes the model and the system but uses stories to highlight and emphasize the various elements of the model. All of the chapters start with a story. Each of the main chapters starts with a short story about a fictional avatar that embodies that particular element or discipline and ends with an example of a biblical hero that modeled the behaviors of that same element or discipline in a Leader Profile. My hope in adding these stories is that they will drive the point home and provide practical examples that you can reference and emulate in your own development as a leader.

Godspeed,

Dr. Thom Owens

Table of Contents

Chapter 1

The Paladin Approach

"Success is nothing more than a few simple disciplines, practiced every day, while failure is simply a few errors in judgement, repeated every day. It is the accumulative weight of our disciplines and our judgements that leads us to either fortune or failure."

– Jim Rohn

Leadership is a difficult concept to define. It seems that there are as many different definitions as there are people trying to define it. Add to this the practice of adding a different adjective in front of it such as transformational, authentic, servant, noble or inspiring and promoting this as some new or unique form of leadership and it gets even more confusing. My personal position is that if you want to use one of these adjectives to further or deepen the dialogue about leadership, then I'm all for it. If you are trying to use one of these adjectives to sell me on your particular brand of leadership, then I'm not buying it. For example, to offer that authentic leadership is a new form of leadership suggests that there is such a thing as "inauthentic" leadership. If it is inauthentic, then it is not leadership. It is something else. Maybe this is why there is a perceived crisis of leadership in the marketplace.

Throughout this book our shared understanding of leadership will come from the Scriptures and the explanation and example of Jesus. In Matthew 20: 25-28 (NIV) we see that Jesus reminds His disciples of the world's standard for leadership. He describes worldly leadership in hierarchical, positional, transactional and contractual terms and follows it up in verse 26 with the command of, "Not so with you" meaning that leadership should be spiritual, servant, transformational and covenantal in its application within the Kingdom of God. Jesus redeemed and modeled leadership for us and in that example guides us to success. The challenge we face today is walking worthy of our calling by refining our understanding of leadership in light of the example of Jesus. The approach we are going to use to keep that understanding in front of us and the model or framework at the heart of it is what this book is all about.

***

He stared out toward the horizon, lost in his thoughts. His was a simple if not easy life. He worked each day to pay his bills and take care of his family. He experienced God's provision in his life and was thankful for it. However, he could not help but sense that something was wrong. He was struggling to make sense of what he saw developing around him. He, like many others, went to services and was involved at the church, but during the week, he just put his head down and worked hard. Sitting in the pews at church he counted himself as one that was willing to join the call to arms to defend against the evil in the world and advance the Kingdom of God. But then came Monday and that willingness got overwhelmed by other demands on his time and energy. This is the pattern that he had fallen into.

Unexpectantly, he was having trouble not with the evil that was "out there" but rather with the presence of evil from within. It seemed like evil was corrupting everything he once thought was good. He saw merchants and shop keepers who professed to know Jesus, cheating their patrons and each other. He saw clergy behave in less than honorable ways. He saw his own leaders abuse their positions for their own material gain and even his peers seemed to be waiting for a chance to take advantage of him or each other in some way.

It seemed that integrity and honor were no longer treated as virtues toward which one should aspire. The words looked good mounted on the walls as if the presence of the words themselves was sufficient. No one seemed to be called to live their lives by them. More and more, these words were mocked and derided so maliciously that it caused some to abandon them as undesirable. Lies and falsehoods were common place and truth was pronounced relative and situationally dependent so as to have no meaning. Darkness seemed like it was everywhere, constantly pushing at the edges of the light, trying to overtake it. He knew this was not right but until lately, he had not been negatively impacted by it. He used caution and counted himself knowledgeable enough, wise enough and strong enough in his faith to navigate the darkness without letting it affect him. He was wrong.

He could no longer just sit back and do nothing, hoping the darkness would not come for him. He felt like he was supposed to do more and be more in the battle that was raging before him. The call to arms was building, stirring his spirit to action. His conviction to fight back was strong, but he did not know what to do or where to go for the answers to his questions. He attended church services regularly and was active in his church, but he came to realize that the brick and mortar building was confirming his feelings that something was wrong but was not addressing what he was supposed to be doing about it. His faith in the Lord was his strength and shield, but this fight against the darkness was going to require deep roots. His limiting beliefs until now had been holding him back, but he became convicted by the Spirit that he had to act. He decided he was going to need help and began to seek answers to his questions.

In all the chaos swirling around him, there was one group of warriors answering the call to arms who seemed to be weathering the storms of life. These warriors were the Knights of the Citadel of Peace, known as Paladins. The Paladins were different from others in that they possessed a confidence in who they were as redeemed children of God, in what is their individual and corporate purpose to advance the Kingdom of God. and in the authority in which they fulfilled that purpose.

Courageous men and women of God joined their ranks to grow in their faith with others who shared their values and desired to become the best versions of themselves that they could be. He decided to seek out the Citadel of Peace to become the best version of himself that he could be because his family deserved his best and he believed that God desires our best effort in the pursuit of Him and His Kingdom. This was Trevelyan's experience and the common experience of each of the Knights of the Citadel of Peace.

***

Paladin Approach Leader Development System

The Paladin Approach Leader Development System is born out of my own challenges as a leader and my own quest to become the best version of myself as a leader that I can be. My hope is that I can serve as your guide on this journey of personal development as a Christian leader. But first let me explain why the "Paladin" approach. The word "Paladin" traces its roots to the Latin *palatinus* referring to the Palatine Hill in ancient Rome and referred to a servant or official from the Imperial palace there.[1] This idea of being a servant is at the heart of leadership and serves as a reference point for us. The word Paladin can be traced to a reference to the Twelve Peers of Charlemagne's Court from 13th century French literature.[2] These Paladins were the warriors that became the epitome of Christian valor in the defense of Europe in the late 8th and early 9th centuries. Of course, the exploits of Roland, Oliver, Bishop Turpin, and the rest are all romanticized stories mostly based on real men. There are also heavy comparisons to the contemporary English stories of King Arthur and his Knights of the

Round Table. Since then, the term Paladin has become synonymous with any chivalrous hero.

I use the term Paladin to define any Christian leader who is valiantly engaged in the difficult journey to become the leader they have been called to be. John Eldredge in his book, *Epic*, encourages us to be the heroes of our own epic quest and not merely a bit player in someone else's comedy or tragedy.[3] Sometimes it is difficult to see ourselves as the hero of our own stories but that is what we should strive for in our daily adventures. We should see life as an adventure to face with bold anticipation, not as a drudgery that we seek to avoid in apprehension. This is our daily choice and Paladins seek adventure in the crafting of their own story. It has been said that the best way to ensure your own success is develop a plan and follow it. This is what I mean by crafting your own story. Story is an important component of who we are and how we ascribe meaning to the world around us. What we tell ourselves about ourselves matters because this becomes part of the narrative of our lives.

As with the first, in each of the following chapters of this book you will read the story of fictional characters that serve as avatars for the various disciplines within the model. It is my hope that through their stories you will see yourself and seek to embrace those disciplines within your life and they will become part of your story. These avatars are known collectively as the Knights of the Citadel of Peace. Their unique names carry meaning and their stories offer a deeper connection to the discipline that they represent.

At the end of each chapter is a leadership profile for a biblical hero that also exemplifies some aspect of the model. Included in that profile is a list of daily actions that you can incorporate into your development plan should you so choose. After you finish this book you will have the baseline knowledge to develop your own personal development plan called a Paladin Action Plan. If you are interested in learning more about or would like some help with your developing your plan visit my website www.strategicinfluencealternatives.com.

As leaders, we should all aspire to be better leaders. I don't know of very many good leaders who are content with the status quo or think they have "arrived" in their leadership journey. The call to leadership is a never-ending pursuit of excellence. To be a better leader is a life-long aspiration. This aspiration comes from our motivation to be the best versions of ourselves that we can be and not from selfish ambition. We call this pursuit of excellence along the path of discovery the Aspirant's Journey. To be clear, this journey is not without hardships. In learning to lead yourself well you will have to grow and stretch beyond your comfort zone. Old habits and ingrained limiting beliefs will have to be deconstructed and examined before new patterns of thought and behavior can be developed. This is also a spiritual endeavor and a call to arms to engage in the battle to be the best version of yourself that you can be. At the conclusion of our time together you will have a choice to make. Will you embrace your calling as a leader and begin the journey of discovery toward becoming a Paladin? Will you accept the challenge of living a life in pursuit of the things of God? It is my prayer that you accept this challenge, continue reading and let me be your guide on your quest.

The Aspirant's Journey

The Paladin Approach is a life lived in pursuit of the things of God and advances the Aspirant through three progressive levels, much like Roland and the Twelve Peers. Stories of medieval knights describe how they progressed from Page, Squire, and Knight just as we must do before becoming a Paladin. We must learn the building blocks of what it means to be a warrior. Make no mistake, embracing the life of a Paladin requires the attitude of a warrior. You must accept that this kind of life is one of growth and development and to do that means that you must be actively involved in training yourself for this life. The Aspirant's Journey requires that we learn one set of attitudes, skills and behaviors before we move to the next level, so let's examine what each of these levels mean for us as learning, growing leaders.

The Page

For the Page, it is all about pursuing Knowledge of God. When do we find God? Jeremiah 29:13 tells us we find Him when we search for Him with all of our heart. So, the motto of the Page is *Cerca Trova*, commonly translated as, seek and you shall find.[4] The symbol of the page is the parchment and pen, signifying the diligent pursuit of knowledge of God through his written

word. The mantle around the scroll and pen represents the mantle of leadership that the Aspirant is training for in their pursuit of the knowledge of God. The border around the banner is Silver Gray, representing the Word of God.

This is where all Paladins start – in pursuit of knowledge of God. This search is the basis for the wisdom that will mark you as a Paladin later in your journey. Proverbs 18:15 (NIV) tells us, "The heart of the discerning acquires knowledge; the ears of the wise seek it out." The scroll and pen serve as a reminder that leaders are learners. I also recommend that you add to your tool kit a Bible, a daily devotional and a journal to record your development. Additionally, there are countless good books that you should commit to reading and studying the themes and principles within, as well as podcasts and blogs produced by other believers. I highly recommend that you visit www.leadershiphunt.com for various articles, blog posts and other free resources to assist you on your Aspirant's Journey. Although the Bible is God's primary communication tool, it is not the only way He speaks to us. He can also speak to us through the words of brothers and sisters within the body of Christ. The role of the Page is to pursue knowledge of God with all of our heart. It is at this level that the rest of the book is focused, but I want to share all the steps of the Aspirant's Journey before digging deeper into the Citadel of Peace.

The Squire

For the Squire, the focus is in pursuing the armor of God. In Ephesians 6:10-17 (NIV) we are given the elements of the armor of God that include the belt of truth, the breastplate of righteousness, feet fitted with the readiness that comes from the gospel of peace, the shield of faith, the helmet of salvation and the sword of the spirit. These items of military equipment were what made the Roman occupying army that the Apostle Paul was referencing the most formidable fighting force of their time. The combination of complete and standardized equipment; belt, breastplate, shoes, shield, helmet and sword, was what separated them from other armies of the era.

At this level the Aspirant is charged with standing in defense, not charging headlong into battle. Therefore, the motto of the Squire is *Nec Temere Nec Timide,* Neither Reckless nor Timid.[5] The symbol of the Squire is the shield with a cross representing the defensive nature of the level and of your faith. The mantle around the shield represents the mantle of leadership that the Aspirant is training for in their pursuit of the armor of God. The color around the border of the banner is green signifying growth as you continue to mature in your understanding of your role in the spiritual fight you are in as a Christian and rebirth from old ways and an old life into new ways and a new life as a Paladin – the leader you are intended to be.

Too many Christian leaders want to use the truth, their righteousness, the gospel of peace, their faith, their salvation and the sword of the Spirit as offensive weapons, flailing about wildly, beating people with their piety and "religiousness." All of these tenants of our faith are likened to defensive equipment by the Apostle Paul, not weapons. Even the sword of the Spirit, at this point in your development should only be used defensively, for blocking the attacks of our spiritual enemy, just as Jesus used Scripture to fight off the temptations of the devil in the wilderness. Not even the sword of the Spirit should be used as an offensive weapon against our fellow man.

The Knight

For the Knight, the focus is in pursuing the weapons of God. In 2 Corinthians 10:4 (NIV) we are reminded that our weapons are not of the world and that they have divine power. At this stage the Aspirant is charged with learning how to use those spiritual weapons effectively in the spiritual fight to which they are called as a Paladin. Their motto is *Incepto Ne Desistam*, May I Not Shrink from  My Purpose.[6] The symbol of the Knight is the array of weapons, sword, axe and mace, representing the offensive nature of the level. The mantle around the weapons is the mantle of leadership that the Aspirant is training for in their pursuit of the weapons of God. The color around the border of the banner is red signifying the blood of salvation and atonement. It also represents the "wounds" you are likely to encounter as you actively engage in the spiritual fight of a Paladin.

As you continue to develop as a Christian leader you will notice two things. First, your efforts at this point will not go unopposed and you will more readily recognize those attacks for what they are when they come. Second, you will be ready for the fight when, not if, it presents itself. The fear that is sometimes depicted in stories of soldiers going into their first battle will be replaced by a confidence that comes from being well trained, knowing what is about to happen and being prepared for that reality. A word of caution is in order at this point. The level of training and readiness that we are talking about is not a casual thing. You are not being called into the National Guard or the Reserves where in times of peace you only train one weekend a month and two weeks a year because you have another job. No, this is a calling to active duty in a time of war that must become a way of life for you. The role of a Christian leader requires more than going to church at Christmas and Easter. It requires ordering your lifestyle around your development as a leader and the pursuit of your purpose. There is a sign at the entrance to the US Army's Ranger School at Fort Benning, Georgia that reads, "Not for the weak or faint hearted." Neither is the call to become a Paladin. But, if it was easy, everyone would do it.

The Paladin

Once the Aspirant completes the previous three levels, they progress to the level of a Paladin. Here the focus is on pursuing the will of God for our lives. In Matthew 16:18 (NIV) Jesus tells Simon Peter, "And I tell you, you are Peter, and on this rock, I will build my church and the gates of Hell shall not prevail against it." We are the church, the ecclesia, the called-out ones – set apart and distinguishable from the rest. We are different, and our understanding and practice of leadership is different. Because of this, the motto of a Paladin is *Praesis Ut Prosis, Ne Ut Impresse*, Lead to Serve, Not to Rule.[7] The symbol of the Paladin is the white knight chess piece. White to symbolize the virtue and valor of a warrior for Christ and the knight chess piece, with its ability to maneuver obliquely around the board, changes the game from one of linear attrition to one of complex strategy. The mantle around the chess piece represents the mantle of leadership that the Aspirant is training for in their pursuit of the will of God for their lives. The color around the border of the banner is blue representing service to God for as believers we are called to be priests in all aspects of our lives.

It is important to note that the life of a Paladin is a commitment to the pursuit of excellence. The journey to be the best version of yourself that you can be, to become the leader you are meant to be, is a lifelong journey. It demands that the Paladin be actively involved in all three aspects of the Aspirant's Journey. You must constantly seek knowledge of God, study the use and function of the elements of the armor of God and develop proficiency with the weapons of God. All of this takes time and training within the Citadel of Peace.

The SWORD of Leadership

Initial Assessment

As a way to at least subjectively assess our baseline level of awareness, complete this initial assessment of some of the main topic areas. At the end I will give you the opportunity to take the assessment again and you can see if your understanding of leadership has changed after our time together.

Indicate your agreement with the following questions on a 5-point scale with:
1= completely disagree, 2= disagree, 3=neither agree nor disagree, 4= agree, 5= completely agree:

1. I am a disciple of Christ, not just a follower, and as such, I am striving to become more like Christ by submitting to the Lordship of Jesus over my life. ☐

2. I know my God-given purpose in life and how I have been gifted to fulfill that purpose. ☐

3. My character and what I value are consistently reflected in my attitudes and behaviors toward others. ☐

4. I embrace all aspects of the spiritual discipline of stewardship in the service of others because I believe that everything I am and have belong to God. ☐

5. I practice the celebration of worship in all areas of my life, thanking the Lord and demonstrating my gratitude as He blesses me in all areas of my life. ☐

6. I accept the twin disciplines of responsibility and accountability, committing to take ownership of my life, my choices and the consequences with authority. ☐

7. I display the light of Christ in the way that I love others as the standard for all my relationships. ☐

8. I incorporate the responses of trust and obedience required of a disciple into all aspects of my life and work as I do my part to fulfill the Great Commission. ☐

Total Score: ☐

11

Don't worry about the total now. The goal is to increase our awareness and the desired outcome is that the score improves at the end of the book as a demonstration of that growth. As we discuss each of the elements of the Citadel of Peace and specifically the SWORD of Leadership, I may challenge you to consider some underlying assumptions about each of these statements. Being open to considering new ideas or becoming more grounded in what you believe are equally acceptable outcomes for someone as they consider embracing the life of a Paladin. As we will discuss, it is not a life of ease. You are going to get uncomfortable if you are growing as a leader.

As a Paladin you will learn the importance of the Citadel of Peace as a model for living the life of a Paladin and how to wield your SWORD of Leadership in pursuit of God's will and advance His glory throughout all creation. What makes this model different is that it is not just another leadership fad. It is the heart of a system that you can order your life around that cuts through the noise and the chaos of life and lets you focus on a set of critical behaviors that allow you to operate within your purpose. When you are operating within your purpose and master the disciplines within this model you will be more effective as a leader, having a greater impact within the Kingdom of God. Let's take a look at the model at the center of the system.

Chapter 2

The Citadel of Peace

"Peace is a daily, a weekly, a monthly process, gradually changing opinions, slowly eroding old barriers, quietly building new structures."

- John F. Kennedy

Are you holding on to the promise of God from Jeremiah 29:11 where He promises that He has a plan for you, a plan not to harm you but to prosper you, to give you a hope and a future? Are you excited by the idea that there is a God-sized purpose for you in this life that should fuel your God-sized hopes and dreams? How many of us really have any idea how big is a God-sized dream?

If you are still waiting for God to deliver on that plan to prosper you, have you ever considered that He loves you too much to give you a God-sized dream all at once if you don't have the life infrastructure in place to handle it? That was where I was and that is what this model represents – an infrastructure to handle a God-sized dream.

***

As he arose from his morning routine that included reciting the Paladin's Prayer, he reflected on what he had been learning since coming to the Citadel of Peace. He had searched for this place for some time and although the Paladins were eager for him to join their ranks, they wanted to be sure that he possessed the courage of his convictions. Before he could truly join them, he had to demonstrate that he was serious about the journey. They cautioned him that it would be difficult, but also encouraged him that it would be worth it.

His biggest challenge when he first arrived was overcoming his limiting beliefs. The enemy had filled his head with lies about who he was and what he was capable of and his teachers showed him the truth of who he is as a child of God. They taught him that for him to achieve his purpose, he would have to change his mindset, to renew his mind to overcome the tension that the limiting beliefs of his past were placing on his current reality, anchoring it in place. He would have to learn to embrace the daily disciplines that would help him pull up that anchor stake and move him toward the future that he has been promised by God.

He took a series of assessments that helped him determine his baseline understanding and core beliefs about the disciplines they were teaching him. They helped him uncover the gifts that he had been given by the Holy Spirit and what his natural strengths are as precursor activities to discovering his purpose. Now that he understood his purpose in the context of serving others, he was on to learning about the daily disciplines he would need to master to renew his mind and become a Paladin. He learned that within the Citadel of Peace the Paladin finds wisdom and prudence. By studying Proverbs 8:12-14 (NIV), he learned that together wisdom and prudence possess knowledge, discretion, fear of the Lord, counsel, sound judgement, understanding, and power. The goal of the Paladin is to gain for himself or herself these seven possessions of wisdom. He came to recognize that the Citadel of Peace is a place for the Paladin to seek his or her spiritual center and learn how to harness the power of the Holy Spirit to achieve their purpose.

From this spiritual centering the Paladin can complete the mental, emotional and physical training that is necessary to successfully engage in the battle they are called to. He was learning more everyday about what it means to abide in Christ and to trust in Him. He learned that without a solid foundation based on his relationship with Jesus, he would not be as effective in his purpose and follow-on efforts to beat back the darkness. He learned that the Paladin's efforts alone are not enough. It is the dependence on the Lord that is the key outcome of Trevelyan's time in the Citadel of Peace and the one that allowed him to become the leader of the Knights of the Citadel of Peace.

***

As mentioned earlier, this system is born out of my own challenges as a leader. I was at a point where I was holding on to Jeremiah 29:11 (NIV) and the promise that God had a plan for me to give me a hope and a future. As I was not so patiently waiting for this plan to materialize I finally in desperation asked the question "When?" As I have already said, the answer I got to that question was, "the God-sized plan I have for you would crush you if I gave it to you now and I love you too much to do that to you. You don't have the life infrastructure in place to hold up the plan I have for you." I was too busy focusing on the fact that there was a plan and I did not know what it was. How can I execute the plan if I don't know the plan? God is focused on me and my reliance on Him for the plan.

However, holding on to Jeremiah 29:11 and knowing that the Lord has plans for you is only half of the formula. Our part in this arrangement is to call upon the Lord in prayer and He will listen to us. The rest of the formula requires us to listen to Him. We must seek Him with all of our hearts. Jeremiah 29:13 (NIV) tells us that when we seek Him with all of our hearts, then we will find Him. *Cerca Trova* – Seek and You Shall Find. Finding is reserved for those who seek. Be a seeker of God and do so with all of your heart and you will find Him and be a part of His plan to fulfill His promises for you and your life.

Even after a career in the military and after over 10 years in the corporate world, I was not ready to step into my purpose and walk worthy of my calling. I still had work to do. I set out on a journey to build the life infrastructure to handle the God-sized hopes and dreams for my future; an infrastructure that focused me not on asking the right questions, but rather how to better listen for the answers. From those efforts came this model - the Citadel of Peace.

The Citadel of Peace

Why the "Citadel of Peace?" A citadel is a fortress or stronghold where one can take shelter from danger, typically on high ground that is more easily defended.[8] Peace is defined as freedom from disturbance; quiet and tranquility; a state of security, free from war. Another definition is the stress-free state of security and calmness that comes when there is no fighting or war, everything co-existing in perfect harmony and freedom.[9] For our purposes the Citadel of Peace is that core fortified area of your life, free from the stresses of your spiritual war, where you train for the life of a Paladin. The Citadel is not a physical place. It is a spiritual place that involves spiritual, mental, emotional, and physical activities.

To enter the Citadel of Peace is a conscious choice to engage in the activities that become opportunities for God to work in our lives. This choice is one of the indications of wise spiritual training which acknowledges this season of your life as an Aspirant. It requires the dismantling of old barriers and the building of new structures, especially when considering our mindset and what it means to embrace Romans 12:2 (NIV) and no longer conform to the patterns of this world, but to be transformed by the renewing of our minds. We also find in Romans 8:5-6 (NIV) that those who live in accordance with the Spirit, with a mind set on what the Spirit desires and one controlled by the Spirit find life and peace.

Other indicators are that it allows the Spirit freedom to move and work on us and our unique gifts as we transit the highs and lows of the journey. The Citadel of Peace is free from condemnation. We are not judged by the number of times we fail. Failures are acknowledged as opportunities to learn and grow. When we are knocked down, we pick ourselves up and look for the lesson we can take away from that experience and how did our mindset contribute to that outcome. Within the Citadel of Peace, abiding with the Spirit, we can gain a clearer picture and a deeper understanding of how to improve as a leader. Let's take a look at each of the parts of the Citadel and why they are important.

The Foundation: The Lordship of Jesus Christ

This first step in building any infrastructure requires laying a solid foundation. This requires removing the debris of our old lives to make a space for the new. Your foundation requires an abiding faith in Jesus Christ and the indwelling of the Holy Spirit in all aspects of your life, not just attendance at an occasional weekend church service. Christ must be the cornerstone of your foundation that keeps everything else even and level. By abiding in Christ and with the help of the Holy Spirit you will discover and improve your gifts, talents, and skills on this journey.

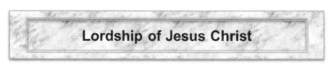

Lordship of Jesus Christ

The Foundation

Your Spiritual gifts are supernatural abilities given to you when you accepted Christ and the Holy Spirit began to reside in you. If you have never taken a spiritual gifts survey or assessment, I highly encourage you to do so. There are several free assessments online and I encourage you to take several. I frequently use http://www.gifttest.org developed by Dr. Dorena Della Vecchio for a baseline assessment of the seven gifts outlined in Romans 12.[10] I'm amazed at how many Christians I talk to that have never tried to discern how they have been equipped by the Spirit by taking any type of survey. Consequently, these are some of the same people who don't really know their purpose and are just drifting along in life trying to get by.

Taking a survey also has the benefit of allowing you to focus on those two or three main gifts that should be the center of your efforts as part of the body of believers. Some people have trouble determining their purpose. Knowing how you are gifted can offer insight into what you are supposed to be doing. It can also allow you to honestly say no to those opportunities that you are not specifically gifted for. On the other hand, I also occasionally meet people who run off a laundry list of their 15 gifts and I think to myself – *leave something for the rest of us to do*. These are also often the same people who burn out quickly because they are not operating in their purpose and trying to do too much, all the while searching for validation and meaning for their lives.

Your talents are those natural abilities that you were born with. Some people refer to these as your strengths and I encourage you to take inventory of your strengths as these too can offer insight into your purpose. Some type of strengths-based assessment is a good place to start and can improve your self-awareness in this area. Some people will tell you to identify your weaknesses and work on improving those areas in your life. My suggestion is to get really good at something you are already good at and become known as that person, not the person struggling to get better in an area in which they have no natural abilities. My only caution to you is to not ignore the Giver of these natural talents. Just like your spiritual gifts, your natural talents or strengths are gifts as well. They should be identified, developed and used for the benefit of others. Hugh Whelchel, Executive Director of the Institute for Faith,

Work and Economics, offers, "The first step to correctly using your gifts and talents is understanding that they are to be used within the context of a moral and virtuous life."[11] This is an important concept for us as leaders, once we accept the mantle of leadership, our lives are not our own. We serve those we lead with the gifts and talents given to us by God.

Next are your skills which are those learned behaviors that are the baseline results of your training, education and experiences. Leaders are learners and we must constantly be looking for opportunities to grow and develop as leaders. This is more than just formal education in school or in pursuit of a degree or a certification. It also includes informal opportunities such as reading books, going to seminars and webinars, and listening to podcasts. Your training, education and experiences are also how you develop your talents and gifts and why you must be an active participant in your own development as a leader. Having an abiding relationship with Jesus must be the foundation of your development plan.

The last elements of this continuum are the results. These results are the outcomes of your development and use of your gifts, talents and skills in the service to others. These are known as the fruit of the Spirit and listed in Galatians 5:22 (NIV) as love, joy, peace, patience, kindness, goodness, faithfulness, gentleness and self-control. These are the results of a life well-lived. These are also the results for which we are held accountable. We should not leave this to chance. These should be the desired and stated results we want and where we are working backward from in the development of our plan to be better leaders. Our efforts to improve require that we be open to feedback and that we must create the feedback loops that are specifically looking at these results, the results that matter. These feedback loops should be an integral part of your Paladin Action Plan which we will discuss throughout the book and the importance of the relationships that give us the feedback we need.

The most important of these relationships and the feedback they provide comes from your relationship with God. My personal belief is that a person comes into a right relationship with and the measure of grace comes through the gift of faith in Jesus Christ. But what does that right relationship look like for one called to leadership? It starts with your foundation. The Apostle Paul tells us in 1 Corinthians 3:10-13 (NIV) that we should be careful how we build, that no one can lay any foundation other than the one already laid which is Jesus Christ. So, we start with our relationship with Christ. If He is not the Master of your life, you are probably not pursuing God's will for your life and you probably don't have a solid foundation on which to build your development plan as a leader. The key to that passage is that no matter what you build, *when* you are tested by the flames, not *if*, that the quality of your work will be shown for what it is. That quality will depend on your foundation.

The Columns: The Disciplines that form the SWORD

Once you have a solid foundation, then you must erect the support pillars or columns that are going to hold up your God-sized dreams. These columns must be strong and positioned well to hold up that dream. The key to having strong columns is that they must be constructed properly to provide the needed support. In our model these columns represent the disciplines we must master if we are to dwell in the Citadel of Peace and embrace the life of a Paladin. These columns represent the disciplines of Stewardship, Worship, Ownership, Relationship and Discipleship and collectively these columns make up the SWORD of Leadership. These disciplines are the focal point for your development as a Paladin.

Our daily disciplines are those activities when repeated consistently, form the basis for the positive habits in our lives. These are not the only disciplines that lead to improvement as a leader, but they are a combination of disciplines that if practiced every day will lead to improvement as a leader. With these core disciplines you have a functional model to order your life around that will help you become the leader you are intended to be, which we will cover in detail in the chapters that follow.

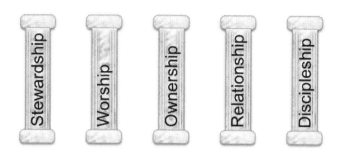

The Columns

The Apostle Paul tells Timothy (1 Timothy 4:7-8, NIV) "...train yourself to be godly. For physical training is of some value, but godliness has value for all things, holding promise for both the present life and the life to come." This training is accomplished through the spiritual disciplines that exercise our spirit which causes us to thirst for a right relationship with God. This keeps our columns (disciplines) evenly distributed along our foundation.

Have you ever wondered how the ancient Parthenon in the Acropolis in earthquake-prone Athens, Greece is still standing after thousands of years? The first reason is that the foundation is set directly on a solid bedrock of limestone. The whole area the Acropolis is built on is one big rock. It has a strong foundation. The second reason is a recent

The Parthenon

discovery. During recent restoration efforts, between the marble drums that form the columns, workers found a square recess carved into the center of each stone, both top and bottom. Set in this square was a block of cedar wood with a hole in the center in which was set a wooden dowel peg. This assemblage of wood acts as a shock absorber and allows the columns to shake without the drums shifting out of position and falling down. These drums were fitted together so well that when they separated the drums the cedar still smelled like fresh wood, even after two and a half thousand years.

Cutaway View

In our model this hidden shock absorber is the Holy Spirit running through the columns that connect our purpose and our foundation. Life is going to jostle you around. The Holy Spirit strengthens your core, absorbs those blows and allows you to keep your disciplines intact and in alignment and in constant contact with your foundation below and the entablature above.

The Entablature: Character (Vision, Values and Virtues)

The next section of the model is the entablature that represents our character. Our character can be defined as who we are when we think no one is looking. However, as Proverbs 5:21 (NIV) tells us, all of man's ways are in full view of the Lord. We should never be deceived to think that we can act in a duplicitous manner, just because we think no one is looking. God is always looking.

The Entablature

The function of the entablature is three-fold, consisting of the architrave, the frieze and the cornice. The architrave or the main beam is the bottom section of the entablature. All buildings are subject to sheering forces that are trying to pull the building down. The architrave keeps even pressure on the columns to keep them in constant contact with the foundation that is supporting them. It keeps the weight of our purpose evenly distributed across all of the supports. This main beam of our character is best described as our virtues. Merriam-Webster defines virtue as a conformity to a standard of right: morality; a particular moral excellence.[12] The pursuit of moral excellence as we practice our daily disciplines is a key aspect of our character and is central to our integrity. God's character is the source of the Biblical standard of virtue and the Holy Spirit is the empowerment of that standard in our lives. Jesus serves as the model or example for us as believers. The moral standard of excellence we seek to emulate is how we conform to the image of Christ.

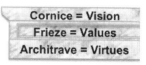

Cornice = Vision
Frieze = Values
Architrave = Virtues

Entablature in Detail

The middle section is called the frieze and in antiquity this section was decorated with colorful paintings or ornate sculptures in relief. This ornamented band has a more decorative function than the other two elements of the entablature. For us the frieze represents our core beliefs and those behaviors that are on display for others to see that reflect our values. Most people have a set of espoused values, but people will know if what you actually value is the same as what you say you value by your behaviors. You can say you value teamwork, but if every chance you get you build yourself up, especially at the expense or to the detriment of others, people will know that you don't really value teamwork. I highlight the decorative aspect of the frieze because it was typically used to tell the story of the building it adorned. Our behaviors tell our story much better than we can articulate it in words.

The final element of the entablature is the cornice. The cornice typically extends beyond the other two bands of the entablature and has the function of deflecting water away from the columns. This represents our vision. Our vision has to extend beyond our daily activities and execution of our disciplines to be effective. No one will follow a leader with a vision that does not extend beyond the current day. Our vision protects our disciplines like the cornice protects the column from erosion. Our vision gives meaning to the difficulties of the pursuit of our purpose. It is hard to endure the price you must pay in pursuit of excellence and the pains of the daily disciplines when the promise is unclear. Our vision tells us and others the promise is worth the price we must pay in the pursuit of excellence.

All together these three elements represent our character which is the basis for and is the critical component to the moral and ethical standard that informs our decision-making. We must have a standard as the basis for those decisions that demonstrates the depth and convictions of our character. Our character, our virtues, values and vision, constitute those qualities that define who we are. For a Paladin, our character, more important than defining *who* we are, tells the world *whose* we are. We are redeemed children of God and heirs to the promises of God.

The Pediment: Your God-sized Purpose

The pediment is the triangle gable found at the front of our citadel. It is the crowning feature of the front elevation of the citadel and represents our purpose – the reason we need the rest of the structure. As noted from Jeremiah 29:11, God has a purpose for every one of us. Our purpose can be described in general terms as our part to play in what my friend Tom Noon calls the divine-human cooperative that God wants us to freely enter into with Him. God has made it known that He wants His glory spread throughout all creation and we are called to join Him in that purpose.

The Pediment

Author Napoleon Hill, in his book *Outwitting the Devil*, notes that this definiteness of purpose is a daily and constant choice that we have to make so that we do not drift through life.[13] This idea of drifting can be described as one of the primary aims of the enemy, to get you to just drift along with the currents of life. To ignore your purpose, let your gifts and talents atrophy and believe his lies that you cannot make a difference are chief among his desires for you. He wants you to keep you from embracing your purpose and advancing the Kingdom of God. To quote Oliver Wendell Holmes, Sr.,

> "I find the great thing in this world is not so much
> where we stand, as in what direction we are moving:
> To reach the port of heaven, we must sail sometimes
> with the wind and sometimes against it, —but we
> must sail, and not drift, nor lie at anchor."[14]

This daily constant choice to set the best sail we can, no matter the direction or intensity of the wind, defines the Aspirant's journey to become a Paladin. Drifting through life is not an acceptable option.

Building a lifestyle of a Paladin requires earnest commitment and a willingness to work hard on each of the areas within the model, especially our relationship with Christ and the daily disciplines of the SWORD of Leadership. It requires the mental and physical development that comes from a lifetime commitment to training for the battles that will surely come to one who follows Jesus. We must commit ourselves to training our minds and bodies within the Citadel of Peace by investing the time and energy needed to make ourselves open to the transformation. We must order our lives around the goal of becoming a Paladin, a warrior for Christ, the leader you are intended to be.

Think of every moment as a potential opportunity to be guided by God and transformed by Him but realize that when you decide to act as a Paladin, the enemy will oppose you. This is why you must spend time in the Citadel of Peace training for those battles. The question that you must answer is this, "Do I possess the courage of my convictions that when my mettle is tested, I will not break and demonstrate the strength of character required of a child of God?" The choice to embrace this lifestyle, training for the battles you are going to face is a decision that is yours and yours alone to make. However, once you make that decision, you are no longer alone. You now have the strength of Christ, the help of the Holy Spirit and the love of the Father to sustain you. You also have me to serve as your guide and other Paladins and brothers and sisters in Christ to spiritually support you on your journey.

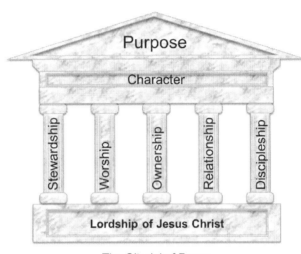

The Citadel of Peace

Awareness of purpose, refinement of character, development of the disciplines and a dependence on Jesus start the journey toward the Citadel of Peace and the calling to become a Paladin. This is the challenge of the call to the life of a Paladin - to take up the mantle of leadership and advance the banner of Christ in all areas of your life. From Matthew 16:18 (NIV) we see that Jesus declares that the Gates of Hell cannot withstand the power and ultimate victory of His church.

As Christians we must stop believing the lie that we are supposed to play defense from inside the walls of our brick and mortar churches. The Gates of Hell are symbolic of a static position of defense. We are the ones who are supposed to be on offense – taking the fight to the enemy. Oswald Sanders in his book *Spiritual Leadership* describes this as "truceless warfare against the devil and hell." He goes on to say,

"Under the Spirit's control our natural gifts of leadership are lifted to their highest power, sanctified for holy purpose."[15] So, my challenge to you is to take up the SWORD of Leadership, refine your knowledge, skills, attitudes and become a Paladin – a warrior for Christ, the leader you are intended to be and advance His banner with your life!

It is my desire that you would take up this challenge and by reading this book let me serve as your guide on this journey. By reading this book you are demonstrating that you are not content to be a bit player in someone else's story and want to be the hero of your own epic quest. Let me encourage you to read on and learn the steps to take on this path to becoming a better leader. By way of further encouragement let me introduce you to a group of heroes who can serve as additional guides along the way.

Knights of the Citadel of Peace

The Avatars

Through the next six chapters of the book we are going to look in detail at each discipline that makes up the SWORD of Leadership. Each chapter begins, as the first two did, with a story. These will each be about one of the Knights of the Citadel of Peace. These knights are avatars for leaders who have struggled with some aspect within each of the disciplines within the SWORD of Leadership. Their stories are our stories. They, like us, started the Aspirant's journey to become a Paladin. Each is a leader that is striving to become a better leader by engaging in the daily battle to improve in each of these disciplines. Like knights from exotic tales, they have unusual names, but each name carries meaning and is part of what makes their story interesting. By way of introduction and their names and associated disciplines are included here. Their stories are told in more detail at the beginning of each of the following chapters.

In Chapter 3 we will meet Joffrey Lévêque. His names translate to "territory of peace" and "overseer." He is known as the Sentinel of the Citadel of Peace. In his story we will see how he struggled with the discipline of stewardship. We will then focus on five elements of stewardship and how it is the expression of our obedience regarding everything God has placed within our care.

Chapter 4 introduces us to Nicolas Clarion. His names translate to "victory" and "call" and together mean the Song of Victory that Brings Peace. This victory song correlates to the discipline of Worship. Nicolas struggles with the discipline of Worship, which is celebrating the daily victories in a way that honors God and acknowledges His Presence in all aspects of our lives. Nicolas learned that practicing the discipline of Worship is pursuing God to the exclusion of all else.

In Chapter 5 we will meet Larissa Navion. Her names translate to "citadel" and "saint." She is known as the Saint of the Citadel of Peace. Larissa often struggled with and eventually overcame her struggles with Ownership. She learned that ownership is accepting the authority delegated to us through Christ and exercising that authority along with the twin disciplines of responsibility and accountability.

Chapter 6 introduces us to Aram Kassar whose names mean "high mountain pass" and "roadway" and translates to Path to the High Road. He learned to redefine his understanding of the discipline of Relationship, which is the way in which people are connected, or the state of being connected. Aram learned that for us, as Christians, the basis of our connections with each other, the path toward the high road, is love.

In Chapter 7 we meet Gerard D'Guerin. His names translate as "brave" and "spear of war" and means Instrument of Spiritual Warfare. We will see how he came to understand the importance of Discipleship, which is following a teacher with the intent of not just following but becoming like the teacher. He learned that is was not enough to just follow Jesus, to be a disciple means that we become like Jesus and lead others to do the same.

Finally, in Chapter 8 we meet again our main avatar Trevelyan DeSerion whose names translate "living on the hill" and "serenity or peace" which means Living in the Citadel of Peace and how being a leader is about putting it all together. At the end of this book you will have a system around which you can order your life in pursuit of your calling to be a Paladin, the leader you are meant to be.

Below you will find the Paladin's Pledge. Here is where you can outwardly confirm your commitment to pursuing the lifestyle of a Paladin. This is for you and you alone. I will never know if you sign this or not, but you owe it to yourself to get the most you can out of this book and this is a way of demonstrating to yourself that you are serious about developing as a leader. The choice is yours, but I hope that you sign the pledge.

Paladin's Pledge

I, _____, pledge to embrace the life of a Paladin by entering the Citadel of Peace and pursuing the daily disciplines of the SWORD of Leadership to become a warrior for Christ engaged in the spiritual battle to become the leader I am intended to be.

_____
(sign and date)

Chapter 3

Stewardship

"When I stand before God at the end of my life, I would hope that I would not have a single bit of talent left and could say, 'I used everything you gave me.'"

– Erma Bombeck

The first discipline of the SWORD of Leadership is that of Stewardship. Often, we equate stewardship to what we do with our money. Our money (and our attitude about money) is important and it is a good place to start because it is easy to count. But it is not the only thing that we should take into account in our desire to be good stewards. It is about so much more as we see in the story of our first avatar.

***

Joffrey Lévêque is known as the Sentinel of the Citadel of Peace. Joffrey is from an affluent family and when he came to train at the

Citadel of Peace to become a Paladin, his wealth was an obstacle to his goals. His teachers at the citadel instructed him about the requirements of the discipline of stewardship but those lessons did not sink in at first. You see, Joffrey had been faithful in tithing exactly 10%, no more – no less, to his local church his whole life. He was under the impression that being a good steward was just about the money. His teachers taught him that he was proceeding from a false assumption. "God does not need your money," they told him. "He desires your heart responding to Him in willing obedience, not duty or obligation." They told him that God desires that he spread His glory throughout all creation and that the Lord had uniquely equipped him to do so. His teachers impressed upon him that his money already belonged to God.

Joffrey learned that Stewards are caretakers, typically of something that belongs to someone else, rather than the traditional hierarchical ruler, governor or positional leader. His teachers explained that the model for this comes to us from Jesus in Matthew 20:26, "Not so with you." In those four simple words Jesus redeemed leadership and cancelled out the legitimacy of all other forms of leadership within the Kingdom of God. In its place He established the only type of leadership that could handle the power and authority of leadership without being corrupted by it, that of a servant. He spent His time among His disciples modeling this new type of leadership by being obedient to God in all that was placed under his control.

Joffrey also thought that his monetary contributions exempted him from other forms of service. He reasoned that he had already done more than many of the other poorer knights. His teachers patiently worked with him through the discovery of his purpose and how he was gifted by the Spirit. Through those exercises they were able to show him that those gifts from God were more important than the wealth with which he had been blessed. Not using his gifts, skills and experiences to advance the Kingdom of God on earth was a poor choice and that money was not a substitution. His teachers had him study the parable of the talents and the story of Nehemiah from the Bible as an example of good stewardship. In his studies he came to recognize that there were five basic elements of the discipline of stewardship that a Paladin must master.

Let's take a look at what Joffrey learned on his journey toward becoming a Paladin.

***

Everything belongs to God. Everything you are and everything you have belong to God. This is one of the fundamentals of our belief as Christians. When we recognize that we are placed here for a purpose, we recognize the importance of being good stewards of everything we have been entrusted with. Dr. Rick Taylor, in his book *The Anatomy of a Disciple* offers that a steward is a house manager.[16] It is fitting that our first area of emphasis as a leader is that of a house manager. From biblical instructions from Titus and Timothy on what makes a fitting leader in the church, there was an emphasis placed on how well potential leaders manage their own houses as an indication of how well they can be trusted to be stewards within God's "house," the church. To be a steward is to be a servant of another. In our role as stewards over God's creation we have from Jesus the example of how to be a servant by nature and not just through positional authority.

To be a steward means that we are sacrificial in our nature, not just in our leadership style, position or roles, or activities or functions. For our discussion, stewardship is an expression of our obedience regarding everything God has placed under our control and the commitment of it all by us to God's service and glory. We are called to be sacrificially generous in our obedience to God.

Just as Joffrey learned from his daily studies of the Bible, we have the Parable of the Talents, where Jesus describes the concept of biblical stewardship. There are some great points for us to consider as we examine how well we are performing as stewards of that which we have been entrusted. Let's briefly review the story, from Matthew 25: 14-30 (NIV):

A man was going away on a journey and he entrusted his property to three of his servants. To one he gave five talents, to one he gave two talents, and to the third, one talent, each according to his ability, and then he left on his journey. The man with five immediately put his money to work and gained five more. The text then tells us that like the first servant, the man who received two put his money to work and gained two more. But the man who received one talent went off, dug a hole in the ground and hid his master's money.

After a long time the master returned to settle accounts. The man who had been given five returned ten and the master replied, "Well done, good and faithful servant! You have been faithful with a few things; I will put you in charge of many things. Come and share in your master's happiness." When the servant who was given two talents presents two more, the master's response was the same, "Well done, good and faithful servant! You have been faithful with a few things; I will put you in charge of many things. Come and share in your master's happiness."

However, when the third servant comes to settle accounts, we get a very different picture. This man said, "Master, I knew that you are a hard man, harvesting where you have not sown and gathering where you have not scattered seed. So I was afraid and went out and hid your talent in the ground. See, here is what belongs to you." And the master was not happy. He called this man a wicked and lazy servant and asked, "So you knew that I harvest where I have not sown and gather where I have not scattered seed? Well then, you should have put my money on deposit with the bankers, so that when I returned I would have received it back with interest." Then the master took what he had given to the third servant away from him and gave it to the first. He then ordered the third, worthless servant to be thrown out into the darkness.

There are many points to consider from this story, but we are going to focus on our stewardship of time, our talents or our gifts, skills, abilities and experiences – those things that make up who we are, our treasure or resources, our temple and our testimony. How we steward these areas are good indicators of and the expression of our obedience regarding everything God has placed under our control and the commitment of it all by us to God's service and glory. Let's look at each of these in greater detail.

 ## Time

The first point from the parable of the talents is about time. In the story, the master is going away for a time and the servants do not know how long he is going to be gone. This reminds us that we do not know how much time any of us have here and of all the resources placed in our care, time is the most finite of them all. Nothing we can do will add one minute to the day, so waiting until tomorrow to do what we should do today is not a good idea. We should constantly ask ourselves, what is the most productive thing I could be doing right now to make the best use of the time I have available. As in the parable of the pounds (minas in the NIV; Luke 19:12-27) author Oswald Sanders reminds us that each servant was given the same amount of money, just as each of us is given the same amount of time.[17] This parable recognizes that we all have different abilities, as the servant with less capacity but equal faithfulness received the same reward. We are responsible for the strategic use of time.

A good steward is also cognizant of time in relation to the past, present and the future. When we review and assess our investment of time, a habit that we should all engage in, we are responsible to learn the lessons from that investment that informs future decision-making. We all make mistakes and bad investments of our time. The real tragedy would be to not learn from those mistakes so ensure that they do not happen again. Too many leaders let the enemy use past mistakes and failures as somehow indicative of their character. Very few leaders set out to make bad decisions. What makes one an ineffective leader is when they do not learn the lessons from that investment of time and they become excuses that hinder their current and future efforts of good stewardship. Don't use it or let others use it as a club to beat you down when you make mistakes. Learn from your past, and make better decisions moving forward.

The present is where the action is and where many leaders get bogged down. As a steward of the time God has given you as a leader, you have to find the balance between learning the lessons of the past, making good informed decisions in the here and now and casting a compelling vision for the future. This is where Peter Senge in his book *The Fifth Discipline* offers that we must manage the creative tension that exists between the past that is anchoring us in our current reality and the compelling vision that is pulling us to our preferred future.[18]

Our understanding of the future and the promise of God from Jeremiah 29:11 and the plans He has for us to prosper and not harm us to give us a hope and a future must be demonstrated as we walk into that future through our faith in Jesus. How many of us have ever uttered the words "I just don't have the time to do the things I need to do" when we are presented with some new demand on our time? Many leaders often face the issue of being led by bottom line pressures. We get fixated on production or meeting deadlines, etc., and we get to the position where we find ourselves sacrificing the important to the tyranny of the urgent.

Peter reminds us in 2 Peter 2:10 (NIV) "For a man is a slave to whatever has mastered him." So, the question is, have you mastered your use of the time God has given you to or has the devil convinced you to drift? The solution to this challenge is to let God lead. Proverbs 3:5-6 (NIV) says, "Trust in the Lord with all your heart, and lean not on your own understanding. In all your ways acknowledge Him and He will make your path straight." I encourage you to let God direct your steps.

Talents

Some translations of the parable of the talents describe the talents as bags of gold or money. The context of the story is that of money management, but it would be a mistake to assume that the story was only about money. In this story, as all parables, the main idea is often a metaphor for something else. In this case the talents represent our gifts, abilities and experiences given to us by God that we are supposed to steward for the good of the body of believers, the church. We are urged to go "at once" and put our talents to work, which makes the connection between our stewardship of time and our talents difficult to separate.

In Romans 12: 5-8 (NIV) the Apostle Paul reminds us, "We have different gifts, according to the grace given us. If a man's gift is… **leadership**, let him **govern diligently** (emphasis mine) …" For those gifted with the gift of leadership reading this book, my prayer is that God increase the measure of grace given to you and that through this book you are given the tools to govern more diligently in your role as a leader.

We are responsible for the continued development of our natural skills and abilities within the time we have been given and for allowing the Holy Spirit to continue to refine our spiritual gifts as God continues to work through us to achieve His purpose for us. That is why reading books such as this one is important to our continued development.

Another element that makes up your talents is in the form of your experiences. God speaks to us through His Spirit, through His Word, through others and through our circumstances. What experiences have gone into making you the leader you are today? This can come through vocation and career experiences at work or in the marketplace, volunteer opportunities at church, a community event or serving in a non-profit organization, hobbies and interests, and entertainment or social groups. Although unpleasant to consider, we are also shaped through tragedy and painful experiences as well. It is important to not get fixated on the circumstances themselves. As spiritual leaders we must be looking for and make the connections between God's activity in our lives and God's character. When we experience God's grace firsthand, it makes it easier to trust Him again, especially when the experience is a difficult or painful one. It is through our experiences where we demonstrate our stewardship in the investment of our time that we also demonstrate our faithfulness to God.

We know that God has made each of us for a purpose and that He has gifted us with certain abilities and experiences to fulfill that purpose and the in dwelling of the Holy Spirit. Paul reminds us in 1 Corinthians 12:4-7 (NIV), "Now there are varieties of gifts, but the same Spirit. And there are varieties of ministries, and the same Lord. There are varieties of effects, but the same God who works all things in all persons. But to each one is given the manifestation of the Spirit for the common good." So, have you determined what your spiritual gifts are and examined how God has used your experiences to refine that gift for the benefit of the body of Christ? I encourage you, if you have not already done so, to take a spiritual gifts survey as a step in that journey.

 **Treasure**

Our stewardship of treasure is perhaps the hardest of all areas to master. Money is discussed second only to love as a topic in the Scriptures because God knows the power that money can exert in our lives. Yet too many leaders misunderstand the warnings concerning money. They misquote the scriptures and claim that money is the root of all evil and reject wealth and profit as evil. This is not what scripture says – it is the love of money that is the root of all evil. Our hearts are the concern, not the money. This is the reason the rich young man could not follow Jesus, not because he was rich, but because his wealth was an obstacle that kept him from following Jesus.

Ken Eldred, in his book *The Integrated Life*, reminds us that Wealth and Profit are biblically affirmed business concepts and no business has ever survived long without them.[19] Jesus even uses these concepts in his teachings, first as we have already discussed in the parable of the talents from Matthew 25 where a 100% return on the investment was sought and delivered by the first two servants, and the third was admonished to have at least deposited the money in the bank to receive interest. Secondly, in the parable of the tenants from Luke 20:9-16 (NIV) Jesus tells of a man who rents his vineyards to some farmers and sent his servant to collect his portion of the proceeds, or his share of the profit. Wealth and profit are affirmed by Jesus. What we must never forget is that this wealth must be managed properly and for the service of others to the glory of God.

Some get confused about what the tithe is and what it is for. They believe that a tenth of everything they receive belongs to God. This is also not true. Everything that they have belongs to God and comes from God. Deuteronomy 8:18 (NIV) affirms that our ability to produce wealth is from God and a way He confirms His covenant with us. He does not need the tithe to advance His Kingdom. God doesn't need the money He gave to us back. The tithe is more in line with what we need. We need a way to demonstrate our obedience to God and tithes and offerings are a way for us to demonstrate to Him that we do not love money more than we love Him. It cannot be our source of faith and trust. When we offer a portion of the wealth that God has given us stewardship over back to Him, it signifies our trust in Him.

Our discussion today is not about the money. It is about determining our attitude about what we value. Do we value our things over God? It is about being sacrificially generous and demonstrating our obedience to God while we are acting as a caretaker of God's things. While we are taking care of God's things, we are expected not just to conserve the present value, but to invest wisely. From Matthew 25:19 (NIV) we are told that when the Master returns, we will have to settle our accounts. When we multiply what we have been given we are good and faithful. We are expected to make a profit. When we are afraid and just worried about the preservation of capital, and do nothing to invest what we are given, just like the final servant in the story – we are considered wicked and lazy. Don't be accused of being lazy when your accounts are settled with the Master.

Finally, we must recognize that God wants us to be successful in all areas of our lives, including financially. But we should not get focused on just the financial part and miss that God measures wealth differently and wants to bless us in all areas of our lives. We are to enjoy those blessings. From 1 Timothy 6:17 (NIV) we see that God "richly provides us with everything for our enjoyment." However, we must never use this as an excuse for over indulgence and forget our responsibilities as stewards of those blessings is to be a blessing to others to the glory of God.

 Temple

Many discussions of stewardship stop after time, talent and treasure. In addition to the main three topics of stewardship, we are also called to be good stewards of other aspects of our lives as Christians. From 1 Corinthians 6:19-20 (NIV), the Apostle Paul reminds us, "Do you not know that your body is a temple of the Holy Spirit, who is in you, whom you have received from God? You are not your own; you were bought at a price. Therefore honor God with your body." As the home for the indwelling Spirit, we must make every effort to take care of our bodies. We must eat right, exercise, and avoid excesses that can negatively impact on our bodies. We must not do anything to quench the flame of the Spirit that resides in us. However, as important as our physical and emotional strength is to our well-being, we must recognize that it is at the limits of ourselves that we run into God's strength.

There is a line in a popular Christian song by Ashes Remain that resonates with me that reveals that we should realize that we are never meant to fight on our own.[20] This has implications for us in our consideration of being a temple for the Holy Spirit. Too often we try to do things in our own strength and relying on our own understanding.

This is not what God wants. He wants us to be in community and partnership with Him. This is why He does not just spell out the plan for us and send us on our way. We would get busy executing and never look back to Him. He assures us that the battle is His, all we have to do is stand firm. Even in Ephesians 6 when we are given the word pictures of putting on the full armor of God, the command is not to challenge the evil one to single combat, winner take all. Jesus already did that and won. What we are commanded to do is merely stand firm. In the context of the stakes of that battle, we got the easy part.

For a less militant example, when we plant seeds, God is the one who makes them grow. We tend to the garden, water it and remove the weeds that try to overtake it and those seeds multiply. God does the hard part and we get to reap the harvest. In both examples, we need God to do the heavy lifting, but God has created a way for us to be a part of the plan because He knows we cannot do the things He created us to do without Him or alone. This is why we have the second area to consider.

Another form of temple is the one of community, common unity with our brothers and sisters in Christ. From Hebrews 10: 25 (NIV), we are urged to meet together and encourage one other as a body of believers through which the Spirit can work in our lives. There is a reason the church is referred to as the body of Christ. There are many parts with different functions to a body. We each have a specific role to play and we need the other parts of the body to function properly. We are formed from community, for community and it is through this community that we wield some of the other elements of the SWORD of Leadership that we will discuss in later chapters.

 ## Testimony

The final area that we must guard and steward properly is that of our testimony. What we say is only half as important as what we do when we profess to be disciples of Christ. People are watching and waiting for any incongruence between who we say we are and who we show the world we are. This is why our values are so important and for us to think of them as the frieze on the entablature or that aspect of our character that is on display for the rest of the world to see. What we say we value and what our actions demonstrate we value must be consistent with our commitments. Our commitment to God should not be taken lightly and our testimony of what He has done for us should be consistent with that commitment. Our walk with God is the outward manifestation of our relationship with Him. When we are working within our purpose and serving others to the glory of God, we don't behave the way the world does.

As discussed previously, God calls each of us to a particular calling to fulfill our purpose. How we act in that calling demonstrates to the world that we are children of God. Jesus said that the world would know we were His disciples by how we loved one another. You cannot say you love someone that you are taking advantage of in a business deal. This does not mean that we let others take advantage of us in an attempt to appear pious. We let our "yes" be our "yes" and our "no" be our "no." It is as simple as that. When we are walking worthy of our calling, we are proclaiming who we are as redeemed children of God and we should strive to protect and actively steward that testimony in all of our dealings with others.

Another area that is important to steward wisely, because it impacts our testimony, is with our family. There is a reason that the instructions from the Apostle Paul for picking leaders in the early churches looked at how a potential leader managed his own house before being picked to serve the church; specifically, how the man interacted with his wife and children. Just as then, today others can get a good indication of our character as a leader by how we treat our family, especially our spouse and our kids. We must recognize that if we have them, our families are gifts from God and we are responsible for managing them in the same way we manage all the other areas we have talked about in this chapter. Managing our calling and our family as part of our testimony are important elements of stewardship and should reflect our desire to serve others to the glory of God.

Summary

In summary, everything you have and everything you are belongs to God. The five areas that I have identified are not meant to be the only areas that you need to address in your application of the discipline of stewardship, but they are a good place to start. In my experience, getting these five correct is hard enough and having a system to order your life around in these five areas will set you apart from those who are drifting through life. If you had to rate yourself on your application of these disciplines how well would you say you are doing in each of these areas? Prayerfully consider and let the Spirit guide your answer to that question.

Your management of your time, talent, treasure, temple and testimony are important aspects of the discipline of stewardship. Below is a self-assessment tool for you to evaluate how well you are doing in each of these areas as a way to increase your awareness and identify areas for improvement on your journey. In the next section refer to the Leader Profile on Nehemiah and use the daily application steps to improve your understanding and development of the discipline of Stewardship.

 **Self-Assessment**

Stewardship: The expression of our obedience regarding everything God has placed under our control and the commitment of it all by us to God's service and glory.

Rate yourself on a scale of 1-5 at how well you are being obedient in the areas of stewardship discussed in this chapter.

	Not at All=1	Somewhat=2	Frequently=3	Regularly=4	Always=5
Time	☐	☐	☐	☐	☐
Talent	☐	☐	☐	☐	☐
Treasure	☐	☐	☐	☐	☐
Temple	☐	☐	☐	☐	☐
Testimony	☐	☐	☐	☐	☐

Leader Profile - Nehemiah: Stewardship (Neh. 1-6)

The Scripture is full of great examples for us as believers to follow and emulate in all our endeavors. From Nehemiah, we see what happens when we follow the blueprints that God has left for us in His word, especially regarding the discipline of stewardship.

In Chapter 1 Nehemiah's heart is broken over what has become of Jerusalem, so he inquires of the Lord in prayer. In Chapter 2 King Artaxerxes notices his sadness and asked what he wants. His first

> *"Like Nehemiah we must be prepared to acknowledge the gracious hand of God when we are moving to fulfill our purpose."*

response is to again pray before answering the king. Our first and continuing question, through prayer, should be focused on whether or not we are operating within God's will for our lives. If we truly believe that everything we are and have belong to God, then as stewards of those things, we should seek out what God wants us to do with what He has entrusted us with. King Artaxerxes looks favorably upon Nehemiah and grants him leave to go to Jerusalem and rebuild the city.

In Chapter 2 Nehemiah went to Jerusalem and the first thing he did was conduct a survey by going out the gate and conducting a 360° assessment of the city walls and all the gates. We need to build in systems to conduct periodic and continuous assessments of our organizations and be prepared to walk around ourselves and inspect the state of our walls sometimes.

Next Nehemiah got buy-in from those who would be helping him rebuild Jerusalem and told them about the gracious hand of God that was upon him. Like Nehemiah, we must be prepared to acknowledge the gracious hand of God when we are moving to fulfill our purpose. So convincing was he that all those he told about his purpose joined him in his good work. From purpose comes success, so we should be clear in our purpose in all that we do.

Enter the organizational antibodies, those with the self-appointed job to attack anything that threatens the status quo. For Nehemiah these detractors were Sanballat, Tobiah and Geshem. These men did not want Nehemiah to succeed, but Nehemiah was clear in his calling and purpose from God and reminded these detractors that they would have no share in what he was building. We too must distance ourselves from our detractors and be prepared to persevere.

"We are created out of community, into community, for community."

In Chapter 3, during the rebuilding of the walls, towers and the gates, the story recounts that there were politicians, priests, business owners and workers involved by name and by profession. Additionally, many of those listed as rebuilding a section of the wall were working near where they lived or worked. This shows that God does not want us to go it alone when He puts something big on our hearts. We are created out of community, into community, for community. God has gifted us all uniquely with individual gifts, skills, abilities and experiences to come together in unity and fulfill the purpose that He has for each of us, especially in the pursuit of a singular goal, as He gave to Nehemiah. When exercising the discipline of stewardship, we must recognize that stewardship means more than just managing financial resources. It means everything God has entrusted to us.

From Chapter 4 we find those detractors who want to see us fail ramping up their opposition. Just as Nehemiah did, we must guard against them and their efforts to stop us and we must confront them with the truth. We are not doing this for ourselves, but for the glory of God. As you become more successful in this pursuit, you may gain the attention of those who might not want you to succeed in your endeavors. We will encounter our own version of Sanballat, Tobiah and Geshem and from Nehemiah's example we know how to deal with them properly.

DAILY APPLICATION

Follow the example of Nehemiah when practicing the discipline of stewardship and:

- Seek God's will through prayer
- Survey the situation
- Recognize that we are created for community and involve others
- Recognize that not everyone we involve will want to see us succeed
- Incorporate biblical best practices into all we do

To summarize Chapter 5, Nehemiah reminds the nobles and officials of the importance of good business practices when dealing with the people, reminding them who they are and where they came from. As redeemed children of God we should establish biblical business practices for dealing with others. The goal should be to inculcate into our business lives the axiom: "Buy from each other. Sell to everyone else." When we do this, we are operating within God's economy and allowing our abundance to bless others and their subsequent abundance to bless others still.

In Chapter 6 there is further opposition to the rebuilding which means that as we start to enjoy success, the opposition will increase. We counter this by being Spirit-led. Therefore, it is important, just as Nehemiah did, to seek the Lord's will through prayer.

When we practice the discipline of stewardship as Nehemiah did, we are operating as we should in God's economy. We have a blueprint for business leadership that we can follow to fulfill our God-given purpose, just as Nehemiah did in the rebuilding of Jerusalem, which he did in record time. Follow the steps in the "Daily Application" and you have a blueprint for biblical success.

Chapter 4

Worship

"It is only when men begin to worship that they begin to grow."

- Calvin Coolidge

The next discipline in the model is that of Worship. Worship is sometimes a difficult discipline to master because of the misconceptions about what it means to worship. What or who we worship is a clear indication of our priorities, our commitments and our values. Worship is ultimately about what we pursue with our time, energy, effort, and money. For our purposes Worship is the pursuit of God to the exclusion of all else. It is about seeking and responding to the presence and purpose of God. Let's see what we can learn about worship from our next avatar.

***

*Nicolas Clarion, the Song of Victory that Brings Peace, comes from a family that attended church services regularly. Nicolas was blessed with an excellent singing voice and he was more than happy to lend his voice to singing in the services at his church. Because of this, Nicolas thought that his singing was all that worship entailed and therefore thought the only time he could worship God was at church. When he arrived at the Citadel of Peace, his teachers taught him that although using his gifts and talents that way was a good start, that was not what it meant to worship God. He learned that worship is the pursuit of God to the exclusion of all else and when he was looking for it, he found reasons to worship God with praise and thanksgiving. He also learned that church was not the only time he should offer praises of thanksgiving and celebration. He was taught to continuously be on the lookout for reasons to celebrate God's goodness in his life.*

The discipline of worship means being in a constant state of praise and adoration to God. He alone is worthy of all our honor and praise. Nicolas came to recognize that prayer, praise and celebration were not just occasional occurrences but rather these should be our continual state of being because of the victory we enjoy in Christ, even in the face of adversity. He was instructed to study King Jehoshaphat and how he, when faced with adversity, chose to sing praises to the Lord rather than be anxious and in so doing found peace. In his studies, Nicolas recognized what it means to pursue God above all else. Let's look at what Nicolas learned on his journey toward becoming a Paladin.

***

Worship is one of those words that too many believers resign to the confines of Sunday morning service that is not allowed to intrude on the rest of the week. But worship is more than that. It is giving God the best that He has given you, deliberately offering it back to Him so that He can make it a blessing to others. It is about communion or sharing with

God. Worship is defined as the feeling or expression of reverence and adoration for God and the show of reverence and adoration for God by honoring Him with religious rites.[21] However, it is more than just the definition as it is both an attitude and an act. All true worship of God is done "in Spirit and in Truth" and takes place on the inside, in our heart or spirit, unfeigned and transparent to the outside. Our praise is rooted in the knowledge of and obedience to the revealed word of God.

We should practice the celebration of worship, thanking the Lord as He blesses us. From Deuteronomy 8:18 (NIV) we see that the ability to produce wealth comes from God and in blessing you so, He confirms His covenant with you. We must remember that when we eat and are satisfied, build nice homes and settle down, when we produce and multiply our treasures, to not become proud and in our hearts forget that this abundance comes from God. Jesus warns against mixing our faith with materialism in Matthew 6:24 (NIV) that "you cannot serve both God and Money."

One of the ways to do this is to adopt an attitude of thankfulness and celebration in all aspects of our lives, including our work and the people we encounter in the marketplace. We should be in a constant state of celebration. Worship is a celebration of God's eternal Presence in all aspects of our lives. To only celebrate one day a week is to relegate the Presence of God in your life to one day a week. We should seek ways to celebrate with God in all aspects of our active partnership with Him.

We should look for reasons to celebrate. Our prayers should include an aspect of celebrations. By being in celebration we acknowledge the blessings of God and worship Him. When we celebrate God's blessings in our lives, we are in fact demonstrating our faith by living our faith. Ralph Waldo Emerson is quoted as saying, "Who you are speaks so loudly I can hardly hear what you are saying."[22] That we are children of God should be so evident through how we choose to worship Him that it should overpower what we are saying. The light of Christ should shine through us so brightly in everything we do but especially in how we worship Him, that it forces the shadows to retreat into a very small corner. Through Him we achieve victory over life's challenges – we just have to claim it. Let's look at prayer, praise, celebration and victory in a little more detail.

 ## Prayer

Prayer is the primary way we communicate with and therefore, worship God. This spiritual discipline is one of the ways we make ourselves available to God. It is through prayer that God changes our hearts and shows us what is important to Him. It is through prayer that we demonstrate our willingness to wait on God and His timing in our lives and prepares us to receive the blessings that can come only from him. It is especially helpful when we are unsure what we should do. In 2 Chronicles 20:3 (NIV) we see that King Jehoshaphat did not know what to do so he inquired of the Lord...he prayed. In verse 12 the king admitted he did not know what to do so he kept his eyes upon the Lord. Keeping your eyes upon the Lord is an important element of being the type of leader this book is about. It is not about us, it is about God and His purpose. Prayer is an essential discipline in preparing for the battles you will face while becoming the leader God intends for you to be.

Prayer as a spiritual discipline nurtures and strengthens your inner life and is an invaluable part of the system you must order your life around to become the leader you are intended to be. You should recognize the role that your prayer life plays in your life as a leader. You should constantly pray for those you lead, pray publicly to remind people that they can and should depend on the promises of God. Pray for spiritual growth and maturity, both for yourself and those you lead. James Gillis reminds us in book *The Prayerful Spirit* that we should not treat our prayer life as a ritual but rather as a relationship, one in which Jesus gives us an enriched image of God, telling us to first love Him and then to love others as ourselves.[23] It is through this love that prayer becomes relationship. We will talk about this more in Chapter 6 but it important to note here that without that love our prayers are returned to us as empty words. It is through our prayer life that God blesses us and when we are in His will, we become a blessing to others, especially those we lead.

 Praise

People praise God in many different ways, but it is not the public acts of worship that matter to God. It is the inner motivation that does. Are our actions a matter of false public piety or of true inner thankfulness. Our attitude and our actions must be right because our worship and praise should call attention to the object of our praise and not to us as the worshippers. We honor God in all we do when we are looking for ways to offer up our praise.

As Christian leaders, it is not our job to withdraw from the world and be thankful in private. We are called to rejoice and weep with the world while reflecting the inner light of Christ. By doing what we have been taught to do and, through collaboration without compromise, we can bring those habits of praise and thankfulness to the world. Through praise, our actions call attention to God's glory. It helps remind us to honor God in all that we do. When we praise God, we acknowledge that He is our sovereign God, worthy of all praise. When we attribute worth to God as a child of God, unmerited worth is attributed to us. We can more easily give credit to God for all that we are and all that we possess when we acknowledge and praise His worthiness.

Through our attitudes and actions of praise, we are reminded of the goodness of God. As leaders we should be looking for all the good that is coming our way. Praising God helps us identify those elements of goodness, even in times of adversity or negative circumstances. God is there with you amid your pain and when we align our hearts toward God it makes it easier to see His goodness in those circumstances. We should be like Hananiah, Mishael, and Azariah (unfortunately better known as Shadrach, Meshach and Abednego) as told in Daniel 3:16-18 (NIV), who when threatened with being thrown into a fiery furnace, asserted that God was able to deliver them. Yet even if He did not, they would still worship only Him. They acknowledged that their duty was to praise and worship God alone, independent of their circumstances.

Finally, whatever our attitudes and actions of praise and worship, we are demonstrating our obedience to and thankfulness for God and His blessings in our lives. Being thankful and obedient in the small things often opens us up for bigger things. We discussed earlier the story of King Jehoshaphat it is worth noting in 2 Chronicles 20:21 (NIV) that when he went into battle, he "appointed men to sing to the Lord and to praise him for the splendor of his holiness as they went out at the head of the army." He led his army out with the band giving thanks to the Lord and noting that His love endures forever. They were celebrating the victory before the battle even began because they knew who God was and were relying on Him and praising His name. We should do the same.

 **Celebration**

We should look for reasons to celebrate. By being in celebration we acknowledge the blessings of God and worship Him. As a leader, are you looking for ways to celebrate the minor as well as the major accomplishments that can bring honor to God? We must be careful not to adopt an "everyone gets a trophy" mentality, but we should use celebrations within our personal and corporate rewards systems to acknowledge both the accomplishments of ourselves and others, and the goodness of God in our lives and business.

From scripture we are encouraged to celebrate by praising and commending others but cautioned to make sure that it is in the right spirit and with the right motivations. Our celebrations should be an extension of our acknowledgment of the glory of God. Once you find reasons to celebrate, take the time to publicly celebrate your thankfulness to God. This means that our obedience to God is not all about rules and "thou shalt nots" that leave life boring and bland. This is not what worshipping God is all about. There should be an energy and an excitement that celebration brings out.

Jon Acuff, in his book *Finish*, makes a very valid point we should consider while pursuing our goals and our purpose and that is to include in them the pursuit of fun.[24] Not many people are motivated to pursue their dreams, passions, purpose or even their goals if they only represent the pain. This is not to say that there will not be pain along the way, but that cannot be the only motivator. Also, I'm not advocating that you only do things that are fun. What Jon points out and what I am emphasizing is that we need to look for the fun in or for ways to make fun what we already have to do to accomplish our goals. Find the joy in what you are already doing and have fun and it will make the journey easier both for us and for others. Too many people, believers and non-believers alike, think that the God we worship is a strict disciplinarian who does not want us to have fun and celebrate the abundant life He has provided for us. This simply is not true.

Another reason to celebrate and to do it with others is that it demonstrates that you value them. Fred "Coach" West, in his book *God's Business*, offers that by including frequent celebrations into your work week you take your people beyond Level 1 (Material) and Level 2 (Investment) motivations and into the higher, more successful motivators of Level 3 (Relationship) and Level 4 (Allegiance).[25] This mutually beneficial and unique environment means that both the people and the organization are committed to the success of the other by rewarding and celebrating those qualities that represent specific qualities and principles. When you treat others in a way that they feel valued, you are demonstrating your thankfulness to them and to God for their contributions and His provision. We also show them that not all of our goals are boring and that all of our motivations are based on fear.

Mike Klausmeier in his book *Corporation Reformation*, reminds us that since our purpose is a God-sized purpose it can appear overwhelming and therefore we should monitor our progress regularly and celebrate our accomplishments often.[26] The achievement of smaller goals along our path of purpose increases our belief in our own abilities and the faithfulness of God. As we begin to experience overcoming those obstacles in our path, we recognize that even our temporary setbacks are opportunities to refine ourselves and our strategies to achieve our purpose. When we celebrate, we are acknowledging the goodness of God in our lives.

 ## Victory

Our victories over our struggles in life should be a source of joy for us. When we rely on our own strength we sometimes fail. When we acknowledge that we can do all things through Christ who strengthens us, we are acknowledging the victories are His and that our gift is not just in the victory or overcoming the obstacles but also in the resulting joy that follows. We have to find and hold on to that joy because all victory comes at a price; a sacrifice we have to be willing to make before we can enjoy that victory.

The reason that this is easier for us as Christians is that Jesus already paid the ultimate price to secure the victory of life over death for us. However, as Christians we are called to make ourselves living sacrifices as an act of worship. Romans 12:1 (NIV) reads, "Therefore, I urge you, brothers, in view of God's mercy, to offer your bodies as living sacrifices, holy and pleasing to God – this is your spiritual act of worship." So, what does this mean to us as leaders? It means that in our quest to be Paladins, the spiritual struggle to be the leaders we are called to be, that there are going to be obstacles that require sacrifices on our part. We cannot hold on to what the world values, so we must let those things go in order to follow Jesus and fulfill the purpose God created us for. We have to no longer conform to the patterns of this world, but rather as Romans 12:2 (NIV) goes on to say, "we must be transformed by the renewing of our minds."

Although it may not seem like it during the struggles against the difficulties you are going to face, it will be worth it as you accomplish the purpose for which you are created. Our understanding that the victory belongs to the Lord but that we are the benefactors of that victory and that we can share in our master's happiness gives us reason to celebrate those victories as acts of worship in all aspects of our lives.

Summary

In summary, what or who we worship is a clear indication of our priorities, our commitments and an outward expression of that which we value. Worship is ultimately about what we pursue with our time, energy, effort, and money. Worship is the pursuit of God to the exclusion of all else. We looked at worship from the position that it is about seeking and responding to the presence and purpose of God and how our attitudes and acts of prayer, praise, celebration and victory are important aspects of that worship.

Looking for opportunities to worship, both individually and with others, and to stretch and to grow in this discipline are the ways for us as leaders to demonstrate that we are endeavoring to walk worthy of our calling. Remember to look for ways to incorporate fun into what you are already doing and release the joy we should all experience as redeemed children of God. This is a joy that comes from knowing that the victory already belongs to the Lord and to us as joint heirs with Christ.

As you take a moment to assess yourself against the standards for this discipline, it may be helpful to subdivide your responses to demonstrate possible disparity between how you worship in a formal church service over how you worship at work or during the rest of the week. By isolating how you are currently practicing prayer, praise, celebrations and victories, in those two settings, hopefully you can reconcile any disparity between the two into a more integrated understanding of how to increase your use of worship in your development as a leader. Prayerfully consider and let the Spirit guide your answers to each of these questions. It is our hope that this chapter raises your awareness of each of the areas of worship and allows you to focus on ways to improve your scores on your journey of becoming a Paladin.

Self-Assessment

Worship: Celebrating the daily victories in a way that honors God and acknowledges His presence in all aspects of our lives by pursuing God to the exclusion of all else.

Rate yourself on a scale of 1-5 at how well you are being obedient in the areas of worship discussed in this chapter.

	Not at All=1	Somewhat=2	Frequently=3	Regularly=4	Always=5
Prayer	☐	☐	☐	☐	☐
Praise	☐	☐	☐	☐	☐
Celebration	☐	☐	☐	☐	☐
Victory	☐	☐	☐	☐	☐

Leader Profile – Jehoshaphat: Worship (2 Chron 20)

When faced with adversity, what seems at the time like an impossible situation, there is a formula for getting through it. It includes the discipline of Worship, the honoring of God above all else. From Scripture, 2 Chronicles 20, we find King Jehoshaphat of Judah faced with a seemly impossible situation and how he got through it. When news of an impending attack reaches him his first response is to inquire of the Lord through prayer. If we are honest with ourselves, how many of us can say that is always our first response to adversity? The scripture tells us that he is both alarmed and resolved in the same sentence. His first prayer was not, "why is this happening to me?" but rather one of resolved inquiry. He was resolved to be within God's will and obedient. He proclaims a fast for all of Judah. This proclamation brought all the people together in their collective resolve to seek the Lord and His will. As leaders we have to be like King Jehoshaphat and inspire others. Those who follow us take comfort when our actions inspire them to right action especially in the face of adversity.

The people assembled, came together to worship before the Lord to seek His help and guidance. Then King Jehoshaphat, as the leader, stood and prayed to God. The king states, "We do not know what to do, but our eyes are upon you." He humbled

> *"Those who follow us take comfort when our actions inspire them to right action especially in the face of adversity."*

himself before the Lord and admitted he did not have the answers but that he knew that the Lord had the answers that he sought. When we are faced with challenges and do not know what to do, we should come before the Lord with a thankful heart and worship Him, keeping our eyes focused upon Him.

It is interesting that the story tells us that not only the men of Judah,

"Do not be afraid or discouraged... for the battle is not yours but God's!"

but also their wives, children and little ones. Everyone assembled before the Lord. As a result, the scripture tells us that the Spirit of the Lord descended upon Jahaziel, one of the men of Judah who stood in the assembly. This is the same spirit that resides in all of those who believe in Christ. Jahaziel, filled with the Spirit, says to the king and all who live in Judah and Jerusalem that the Lord says, "Do not be afraid or discouraged because of this vast army. For the battle is not yours but God's!" If we substitute this "vast army" for some other thing we are afraid of or discouraged by, we can draw the same strength knowing that when we engage the Lord in prayer and seek His will that the battle is not ours, but God's! We have access to that same Spirit that gave King Jehoshaphat that encouragement and guidance when we pursue Him to the exclusion of everything else.

Continuing on with the story, we find that Jahaziel continues and again reminds the people of Judah that they will not have to fight the battle, but that action is required of them. They have to take up their positions, stand firm and witness the deliverance the Lord will give to them. Even though the fight is not theirs, they still have to participate and trust that the Lord will do what He says He will do. They have to take up their positions and stand. We see this again in Ephesians 6:11 (NIV) when the Apostle Paul tells us to put on the full armor of God so that we may take our stand and again in v 13 he tells us to put on our full armor of God so that we may stand our ground and after we have done everything, to again stand. The action required of us sometimes is to just stand and stand firm while God does the hard work.

Back in 2 Chronicles 20:21 (NIV), King Jehoshaphat, after consulting with the people, appoints people to sing praises to the Lord and to praise Him for the splendor of His holiness, to "give thanks to the Lord for His love endures forever." Jehoshaphat places these people at the front of the army. By the time the men of Judah took up their

---

DAILY APPLICATION

When faced with adversity:

- Go to the Lord in Prayer and inquire of the Lord

- Humble yourself and admit you do not know what to do, staying focused on the Lord

- Be obedient and lead others in right actions

- Wait for the Spirit

- Recognize which battles belong to God and let Him fight them

- Do your part and stand

- Give thanks to the Lord and worship Him before the battle

- Give thanks to the Lord and worship Him after the battle

- Enjoy the abundance of the blessing

- Know peace

---

positions and looked in the direction of the advancing vast armies of their enemies, all they saw were dead bodies littering the ground. The Lord had already fought the battle, and no one had escaped. All that was left to do was to carry off the plunder, which was more than they could carry.

The plunder was so great that it took the men of Judah three days to carry everything of value away. On the fourth day, they again sang praises to the Lord. From this we can see that when what appears to be adversity strikes, if we seek the will of God through prayer, follow His directions and participate in the plan by doing our part, the Lord will fight the battle and we get to enjoy the things of value. Arguably the most valuable thing that the King received was in v. 30. The Kingdom was at peace for God had given the king rest on every side. Their enemies were afraid of the power of God after this display, for they knew that God had fought the battle. Would your enemies grant you peace if they saw the power of God in your struggles?

Follow the steps in the "Daily Application" and humbly admit that you do not have all the answers but recognize that God does. Practice the discipline of worship with prayer, praise and thanksgiving in your role as a leader and enjoy the victory that is your and the blessings of God.

Dr. Thom Owens

Chapter 5

Ownership

"The price of greatness is responsibility."

- Winston Churchill

One of the greatest challenges I see in developing leaders is the reluctance to take ownership of anything. Very few people want to be responsible for anything, including themselves. Everything that is not going to their benefit is someone or something else's fault. I learned a valuable lesson in the military, especially when I was a company commander. It was a guiding principle that I encountered daily and was the basis for all my decisions and the consequences of those decisions. "I am responsible for everything my unit does or fails to do." As a leader we must own our decisions and their consequences, good and bad. Leaders don't make excuses. They operate within the full limits of their authority, committed to the pursuit of excellence, and they accept the reality of the twin elements of responsibility and accountability that make up the discipline of ownership, symbolized by the key icon. Let's look at how our next avatar dealt with this reality in her circumstances.

***

Larissa Navion, whose names translate citadel and saint is known as the Saint of the Citadel of Peace. Larissa is the only girl and youngest child in her family. Early on in her life she was often granted preferential treatment because she was the only girl. She knew she was gifted as a leader and wanted to develop her skills and abilities, but often used other's willingness to defer to her because she was a woman to her advantage. Later in life, this started working against her as she sought to lead in roles traditionally led by men. She was confused and inconsistent in her desires. Did she want preferential treatment because she was woman or not?  *This stopped when she came to train at the Citadel of Peace. Her teachers taught her that the leadership that was taught there has nothing to do with gender and everything to do with fulfilling the purpose that comes with the gift of leadership. As a leader called by God, she was given authority that she was both responsible and accountable for the use of in pursuit of her purpose. She had to take ownership of her development as a leader by committing herself to that development.*

Her teachers stressed that the life of a Paladin would be hard and that being a woman would not make it any easier or harder. How easy or hard depended on the consistency of her character and her level of competence, not her gender. She was not competing for positions or titles any longer. The battles she would face will not be fair and the enemy would not defer to her because she was a woman. They taught her that God desires that she advance His glory throughout all creation and that the Lord had given her a gift to accomplish this, but it must be developed to be used correctly and effectively. Her teachers had her study the leadership of Deborah from the Old Testament and how she had to deal with other leaders like Barak who did not accept the responsibility and accountability demanded of leaders.

Through her time of study and training she learned how to use the power and authority that comes with the mantle of leadership and to accept the responsibility and accountability that comes with it as well by fully committing to the life of a Paladin. Larissa embraced her role as a leader and became an inspiration for others. She came to recognize through the example of Deborah that accepting the authority of God means to first totally surrender and submit to that authority. She had to commit to embracing the elements of the Citadel of Peace and ordering her life around that system. She became such an accomplished leader that she came to be admired and venerated because of her character and virtue and became known as the Saint of the Citadel of Peace. Let's take a look at what Larissa learned on her journey toward becoming a Paladin.

***

To be effective as a leader means that one has to take ownership of what you are called to lead. To take ownership of what we are called to lead means exercising authority over our lives and the lives of others. Authority means two things, the right to exercise power and the ability to or the actual exercise of that power. There is no authority if that power is not delegated to you and there is no authority if that power is not used. Where does this authority come from? Matthew 28:18 (NIV) reminds us that Jesus said, "All authority in heaven and on earth has been given to me." In enduring the cross and the crown of thorns, Jesus fulfilled all the requirements to redeem creation and us. He is the Lord of Lords and the King of Kings.

 **Authority**

In the exercise of our authority, leaders are responsible and accountable for everything their organization does and what it fails to do in the pursuit of its mission and purpose. As the leader models the boundaries of ownership, he or she must accept the twin elements of the discipline of ownership, those of responsibility and accountability and acknowledge that man's ways are in full view of the Lord and He examines all your paths (Proverbs 5:21, NIV). It requires a level of commitment and consistency in not only what you espouse but also the demonstrated behavior. The question we must ask and answer for ourselves is, "Do I readily accept the ownership of my purpose that comes from being humbly submitted to the authority of Jesus?"

Tom Marshall in his book *Understanding Leadership*, notes that true authority is spiritual in origin as it proceeds from the spirit of the one exercising it and it impacts on the spirit of the person over whom it is exercised.[27] Another point is that since authority is delegated, it can only be used by those who are in an obedient relationship with the source of the power. What is the source of our authority? As previously stated, Matthew 28:18 (NIV) reminds us that Jesus said, "All authority in heaven and on earth has been given to me." Jesus passed that authority to His disciples in Matthew 19:19 (NIV) when he gave them to the keys to the kingdom of heaven. So, what does that mean to us who have been entrusted with that authority? It means that we are held to a higher standard. However, before we can understand the implications of that authority and standard, we have to look at the power that comes from authority.

Power can be described as the capacity or ability to exert one's will in the exercise of control over the environment or others. As we stated in Chapter 3, Stewardship, everything we have and are belongs to God so all power flows from God. In Genesis mankind was given authority over the world God created and as stewards of that creation man was delegated the right to exercise power over his environment. However, in the fall man was tempted to reach for autonomy, to be like God and be the source of his own wisdom and power. In this illegitimate power grab man fractured the perfect peace of God's creation and as a result, God reordered His creation and the ability of man to exercise power over creation. No longer was the direct line between God and man the basis for power, but rather now power was between man and man. This continued until Jesus came to redeem power and leadership.

From Matthew 20:25 (NIV), Jesus reminded His disciples that the rulers of the Gentiles lord their power over them, and their high officials exercise positional authority over them but then in four words redeemed power and leadership, 'Not so with you.' He gave them, and us, the model for who could be trusted with this level of power; one who was not in it for status and who was willing to serve others. For it to be legitimate, you must be willing to submit to the source of your authority – Jesus. Are you in a position of authority over others? You should exercise the power that comes with that authority by constantly looking for ways to serve those you have authority over.

You should not strive for positions of authority just because it gives you power over others. This is not to say that you should not strive for a leadership role. On the contrary, Paul tells us in 1 Timothy 3:1(NIV) that to aspire to leadership is an honorable ambition. The caution is as long as it is done in order to be of service to others. The world does not recognize this kind of leadership for what it is – the true use of redeemed power, but they recognize the results that come from organizations and leaders who model this kind of power and authority – the power and authority that comes from God.

 ## Responsibility

Now that we know that the exercise of spiritual authority comes from our relationship with Jesus and that with that power and authority comes at a cost, we must recognize that we are held to a higher standard. As discussed in the previous chapter, Jesus paid that cost to redeem us, power and the relationship with God from which our spiritual authority flows. But now as redeemed children of God we must strive to conform to the image of His Son. That means accepting that higher standard. We must accept responsibility for our attitudes and actions as we exercise that redeemed power and authority. We must accept that we are responsible for everything that the organization we are called to lead does and fails to do in pursuit of its mission and purpose. This is an awesome responsibility and being under this type of scrutiny is why many shy away from this level of responsibility.

To illustrate the point, let's take a look at what I call the very first recorded leadership failure, from Genesis and the story of Adam. God had delegated His authority to Adam but put some boundaries in place with regard to a certain tree and Adam's behavior related to that tree. And we know from the story that Adam passed this information on to Eve because she was created after this, yet she was the one who informed the serpent that the tree was out of bounds. (I personally believe that the serpent targeted Eve, not because she was the "weaker sex" but rather because she was potentially the one working with second hand information. God told Adam the rules before Eve was around.) We all know that she was tempted and ate of the fruit but sometimes what is lost in the telling of the story was that Adam was standing there when all of this occurred, and he did not exercise his authority as a leader – to disastrous consequences; the first leadership failure.

Then the story continues. God is walking in the garden and asks (I'm paraphrasing a little), "Adam…where are you?"

Who was the question for? God knew where Adam was. We cannot hide from God, but that did not stop Adam from trying.

Adam responds, "I was hiding."

God asks, "Why were you hiding?"

Adam responds, "Because I was naked."

God asks, "Who told you that you were naked? You ate the fruit, didn't you?"

Then the second and third leadership failures. First, he tries to pass the buck to God, "You put this woman here, so it's your fault…" when he quickly realized that wasn't going to work, he threw Eve under the bus, "the woman – she did it, it was her fault." He did not want to own his mistake and take responsibility for his decisions, first, not to stop her and put the serpent in his place, and second not to eat of the fruit himself. At any point he could have told the serpent that they were not going to have this conversation, but he didn't. He could have corrected his wife when she added the "and we can't even touch it" part to the instructions. He could have also taken his wife by the hand and simply walked away…it was a tree after all. But he didn't do that either. One of the harder things to consider, and it certainly was an option, he could have refused to join her in her sin and not eaten of the fruit himself, even if it meant she was banished from the Garden, and he was not. Adam did not take charge of the situation and exercise the authority given to him to be the leader that God intended him to be. It took Jesus redeeming creation and leadership to restore what was lost in Adam's failures.

Another point I want to make is that there is a difference between being in charge of your organization and being in control of everything. It takes a special kind of leader to be able to delegate authority yet maintain responsibility for others. Leaders who can do this demonstrate a level of maturity and humility that is required to be a Paladin and accept this dynamic of delegating authority but retaining responsibility.

 ## Accountability

Being a leader means submitting to the accountability that comes from the source of your authority and accepting the consequences of your decisions and actions. From our review of Adam's leadership failures, we see that not only did he not want to accept responsibility, he certainly did not want to be held accountable for the consequences of his failures. When we continue reading the story in Genesis 3, we see that everyone present was impacted by the consequences of Adam's failures, the serpent, Eve and Adam; even God. While describing the consequences of this turn of events, He included His own Son in the equation to rectify the situation. Because He did, we, and leadership, have been redeemed and the source of our authority restored. It is up to us to continue to develop ourselves as leaders and hold ourselves accountable to the higher standard Jesus has set for us.

Leaders who embrace the ownership of their own personal and professional development, as well as the development of those they lead, accept accountability as a necessary part of the equation and accept the consequences of their leadership. They put processes and systems in place that demand accountability for the consequences of their decisions. They are self-aware enough to realize that they still have something to learn and humble themselves before others, especially those they lead and encourage accountability at all levels of the organizations that they lead. They are spirit-led and are quick to take ownership of outcomes, especially when they are less than optimal. Unlike Adam, the task of Christian leaders is to conform to biblical standards by acknowledging their source and being willing to submit to accountability related to our exercise of authority. Being able to submit to this level of accountability requires a deep commitment to something bigger than yourself, a level of maturity that is often lacking in secular models of leadership and a level of humility that is equally absent.

If we remember back to our discussion of the parable of the talents from Matthew 25, when the master returned the three servants who had been entrusted with the master's property had to give an account. Someday we are all going to give an account for everything we have been entrusted with. It is in our ability to accept accountability that we demonstrate our trustworthiness. To the two servants that demonstrated that they could be trusted with a little, they were given much more for which they were to be responsible and accountable. Klausmeier also reminds us that to be worthy of trust, as leaders we must possess the character of Jesus, a competence influenced by the Holy Spirit and a relational connection founded on humility.[28] With these three things, we are not only willing to be held accountable; we demand it as a demonstration of our ownership of what it means to be a leader and our commitment to our development as a leader.

 ## Commitment

To commit to something is to make an agreement or pledge. To take ownership of our own development as a leader and ownership of our purpose as a leader is not a casual agreement or promise. This level of commitment is what transforms the promise into reality, the pledge into obligation. Like the segment of chain in the icon for this section implies, it binds us to our purpose. Commitment to take ownership of your life and your life's purpose is a serious agreement that should not be entered into lightly. To make this level of commitment to excellence involves a high degree of trust. We have to trust that if we make this commitment that we will gain the positive benefits of ownership. This is how we mitigate the negative consequences of not taking ownership.

For us to embrace the deep change of becoming a Paladin, we are committing to embrace the possibilities of that lifestyle and to adopting the values and beliefs before that change can occur and before there is any evidence that the change can be accomplished. This is more than being involved in half-hearted efforts to improve incrementally. It takes a deep level of commitment to the transformation of our old lives to a new life; a commitment to pursue excellence. I was once asked over a breakfast meal of ham and eggs if I knew the difference between involvement and commitment. It was pointed out to me that the chicken that laid the egg was involved. The hog was committed. We should strive for all-in commitment over detached involvement by trusting in the promises of God.

What are the current barriers to this level of commitment? The biggest is fear. Fear of the unknown, fear of failure, fear of rejection, fear of change and even fear of success can all be obstacles to our commitment and to our ability to practice the discipline of ownership of our lives and purpose. Making this level of commitment to the life of a Paladin inevitably leads to some level of change that upsets the status quo. What if we try and don't succeed? If we are doing the right things, even if we fail, we have to look for the learning that happened and not take failure personal. To uncover the best version of ourselves requires us to step out into the unknown sometimes. It is there that we learn and grow.

Summary

In summary, as a leader we must own our decisions and their consequences, good and bad. Leaders don't make excuses. Leaders operate within the full limits of their authority, commit to the pursuit of excellence and accept the reality of the twin elements, responsibility and accountability, of the discipline of ownership. We looked at the source of our authority and the power that comes with it. We acknowledge that the discipline of ownership is embracing the premise that as a leader you are responsible for everything you do and fail to do in the pursuit of your purpose. We accept that as leaders we will be held accountable for what we have been entrusted with and long to hear the words, "well done good and faithful servant."

As you take a moment to assess yourself against the standards for this discipline, it may be helpful to consider how you model the use of power that comes from your authority over others and how those behaviors will serve as a guide for others to emulate. Examining how you delegate authority yet retain responsibility and implement accountability for yourself and others will help you grow as a leader and demonstrate your level of commitment to your own development and the development of those you lead.

 **Self-Assessment**

Ownership: Accepting the authority delegated to us through Christ and exercising that authority along with the twin elements of responsibility and accountability in our commitment to pursue excellence.

Rate yourself on a scale of 1-5 at how well you are being obedient in the areas of ownership discussed in this chapter.

	Not at All=1	Somewhat=2	Frequently=3	Regularly=4	Always=5
Authority	☐	☐	☐	☐	☐
Responsibility	☐	☐	☐	☐	☐
Accountability	☐	☐	☐	☐	☐
Commitment	☐	☐	☐	☐	☐

Leader Profile – Deborah: Ownership (Judges 4 & 5)

The story of Deborah in Judges 4 & 5 is unique in that it casts a woman in the role of leading the people of Israel. From this we should take that God can use anyone who is willing to accept the discipline of ownership and join Him in His purpose. The story begins in a familiar place with the Israelites doing evil in the eyes of the Lord. When they find themselves in this position, God often allows His children to be oppressed, in this case by Jabin, the king of Canaan, who cruelly did so for 20 years. During this time Deborah, the judge of Israel, holding court under a palm tree, is leading Israel. The Israelites came to her to have their disputes settled, the traditional role of the leader of Israel dating back to the time of Moses. The Lord speaks to her with the answer to Israel's situation.

> *"Even when we find ourselves in a bad situation, God has a plan for His children."*

In verses 6 -7 she sends for Barak and tells him, "The Lord, God of Israel, commands you: 'Go, take with you ten thousand men...lead the way.... I will lure Sisera, the commander of Jabin's army ... to the river and give them into your hands.'" God is in control and even when we find ourselves in a bad situation, God has a plan for His children. In this case, as revealed in Chapter 4, verses 23-24, it was to subdue Jabin before the Israelites and as the hand of the Israelites grew stronger and stronger against Jabin, to eventually destroy him. But, back to the story.

However, Barak (v. 8) said to her, "If you go with me, I will go; but if you don't go with me, I won't go." Now the Scripture is not clear about why this was Barak's response. It could have been that he did not trust in the word of God after having been oppressed by the Canaanites for so long, or he may not have believed that this command came from God through Deborah. It could have been that he did not think the Israelites would follow him without Deborah being present. We will never know the exact reason for his response, but his response reveals that there is a question of ownership of the calling. Barak does not appear to want the responsibility and accountability that comes with his calling from God. How many times is this our attitude when God calls us to share in His purpose?

So, Deborah (v 9) said, "Very well, I will go with you. But because of the way you are going about this, the honor will not be yours, for the Lord will hand Sisera over to a woman." Without getting into the

> *"If you don't want to take responsibility for your calling, someone else gets the honor that comes from completing your tasks."*

cultural nuances of the time, the implication is clear. If you don't want to take responsibility for your calling, someone else gets the honor that comes from completing your tasks. How many leaders have you encountered who want the honor, the accolades, the benefits from completing a task or project, but don't want to assume any responsibility and certainly none of the accountability that comes from owning the mantle of leadership? From verse 14 Deborah, who went with him, tells Barak, "Go! This is the day the Lord has given Sisera into your hands. Has not the Lord gone ahead of you?" Barak had to be reminded that the Lord had already decided the outcome of the day. How many times must we be reminded that the Lord has already gone ahead of us and secured the outcome for us in the things He asks of us?

In verses 15 and 16 we see that all that was required of Barak was to advance, to get started, to demonstrate his commitment and a level of obedience toward God and His purpose and that "the Lord routed Sisera and all his chariots and army by the sword. ... All the troops of Sisera fell by the sword, not a man was left." When we, as leaders, accept the discipline of ownership, we not only get the burden of responsibility and accountability, but more importantly we get all the authority that has comes to us as followers of Jesus. When we boldly advance in our God-given purpose, we have the assurance that comes with that in the form of the all authority granted to Jesus by the Father, that He then passed to us. How less intimidating is the responsibility and accountability of your calling when you know you have the authority that comes from being called by God to join Him in His purpose?

Next, we find that Sisera flees the battle on foot, his mighty chariots do him no good, and he takes refuge in the tent of Jael. There he is

DAILY APPLICATION

Exercising the discipline of Ownership requires:

- Accepting responsibility and accountability

- Recognizing whose authority you are operating in

- Remembering God has gone before us in everything He asks us to do

- Taking the lead when God calls

- Willingly offering yourself, submitting to God's authority in your life

- Recognizing that nothing is impossible for God

delivered into the hands of a woman who, while he is sleeping, drives a tent peg through his temple into the ground. In verse 22, when Barak comes by in pursuit, Jael goes out to meet him and shows him the man he is looking for – dead. In Judges 5, known as the victory song of Deborah, it is the deeds of Jael that are extolled in song, not those of Barak. Deborah told Barak that the honor would not be his, but that it would belong to another – Jael.

Also, from Chapter 5, we see that when God's people take the lead and willingly offer themselves, the Lord goes before them. In verse 20, "From the heavens, even the stars fought, from their courses they fought against Sisera." When God is with you and you are in His will, nothing is impossible for the Lord.

Be like Deborah, one embracing the discipline of Ownership, operating in the Lord's will and with His authority and not like Barak, hesitant and waiting on someone else to "go with you" in your calling. To be the leader God intends for you to be requires that you lead diligently and willingly submit to God's authority - the source of your authority.

Chapter 6

Relationship

"The relationships we have with people are extremely important to success on and off the job."

- Zig Ziglar

Depending on your personality type, relationships can appear to be either the hardest or the easiest of the disciplines to master. However, the perception of relationship with too many people is that it is reserved for a romantic dynamic between two people or a group of close friends. This is not necessarily what I am talking about here. Relationship is defined as the way in which two or more concepts, objects, or people are connected, or the state of being connected.[29] We are going to focus on this state of connectedness. For our understanding of relationship, we are going to look at how our avatar discovered the value of being connected and we are going to study one particular verse of scripture as a guide for the rest of our discussion about to whom we are supposed to be connected.

***

Aram Kassar, named for the Path to the Peaceful High Pass, is unique among our avatars because he is of both Persian and Moorish descent. He wears and uses armor and weapons in the style of his native culture, opting not to adopt those of his contemporaries in the Citadel of Peace. When he became a Christian, he wanted to be a leader that others from his culture would follow on the path or the way that leads to and is Jesus.

However, he did not live up to his peaceful name when he first came to the Citadel to begin his training. He sought offense where none was intended and found offense where none existed. He chose to focus on his difference with the others rather than what unified them – the love of Jesus. This strained all of his relationships with the other Aspirants on their leadership journey. At first, he did not want to develop relationships with others. He was there to develop himself as the leader God called him to be, not to make friends with the others. His teachers taught him and showed him the love of God as the basis for all relationships. They taught him that to be a leader that others would follow meant that he had to foster the type of relationships that were centered on God and His love.

His teachers stressed that the life of a Paladin was not one of solitude or loneliness. As part of the body of Christ, we all have a part to play and that no one is called to the battle with evil to engage in "single combat – winner take all." That task has already been accomplished by Jesus because of the Father's love for each of us. We are designed out of community, into community, and for community and how we love others is a reflection of how we love God. His teachers explained that Jesus taught that the world would know we were His by how we loved one another. His teachers also taught him the lessons of leadership from the story of Jonathan from the Old Testament and showed him how to be a leader like Jonathan that relied on God and inspired others to follow him, even when the situation is dire – because they know that God was with him.

Through his time of study and training he learned how to love God, others and himself in such a way that his relationships became an example for others to follow. He learned to live up to his name and became one that points others to the path of the peaceful high pass. The path that leads to Jesus. Let's take a look at what Aram learned on his journey toward becoming a Paladin.

***

As we saw in our definition, the basic principle of relationship is connection. As humans we seek to make connections between ourselves and other people, places, or things. This can range from a sense of belonging to a particular group, all the way to intimacy. On the one end this sense of connectedness manifests in the world as affinity for sports teams, political affiliations and unfortunately as church denominations. On the other, intimacy according to the world equates to lust. What is missing from the worldly understanding of relationship and what is the central aspect or glue that holds these relationships together is love. The problem we have is that our modern-day culture has twisted the meaning of love into something that it is not. We say we love a certain flavor of ice cream, or we love a particular book or movie, we love our pets, and yet we reserve the word love to something only spoken to another human being at the end of a period of courtship when we have decided that person is "the one."

The expression of love toward others should be as easy as our expressions of love to things, but often that is not the case. From Matthew 22:37-40 (ESV) we get the ultimate expression of what it means to be in relationship:

"And he said to them, 'You shall love the Lord your God with all your heart and with all your soul and with all your mind. This is the great and first commandment. And a second is like it: You shall love your neighbor as yourself. On these two commandments depend all the Law and the Prophets.'"

The first connection is with God, the second is with others and the third is with ourselves. We are to love God with all of our heart, soul and mind. Then we are supposed to love our neighbors, how? – just like we love God – with all our heart, soul and mind. Finally, we are to love ourselves. Many people miss this third aspect of how we are to love. How can we truly love others the way we love God if we do not love ourselves? The way that we love God, others and ourselves is so important Jesus tells us in John 13:18 (NIV) that this is how the world will know that we are His disciples, by how we love one another, just like He loves us. This is an outward manifestation of an inner decision to follow Jesus.

Max DePree, in his book *Leadership is an Art*, reminds us that as Christian leaders in the marketplace our relationships with each other need to tend toward more transformational over transactional and covenantal over contractual in nature.[30] We need to demonstrate our love for God, each other and ourselves at all times – not just when we feel like it, when we think someone else is watching, or when there is something in it for us. As a Christian leader, we should constantly evaluate the health of each of these relationships. Without them, we are not leading anyone anywhere in an effective manner.

 **With God**

It is our relationship with God that defines us as Paladins. To have a personal relationship with Him means that we are seeking His will for our lives. As Christians we believe in one God, but that He manifests in three separate persons. Some say that God the Father, plus Jesus the Son, plus the Holy Spirit equals God. Mathematically this is $1+1+1=1$

but this is not accurate. 1+1+1=3. A better way to understand this is that Jesus and the Holy Spirit are not additive, but rather magnify who God is, glorifies God and should be expressed as 1x1x1=1.[31] This is mathematically accurate and more in line with how Scripture treats the central tenet of "One God in Three Persons." The Trinity or the Triune God are labels we use to help us understand a very complex dynamic yet are not specifically used in Scripture to describe God. For us to understand the importance of this discipline, let's look at our relationship with all the manifestations of God a little deeper.

The foundation of this as we have already discussed is our relationship with Jesus because no one comes to the Father, except through the Son. Jesus calls us not to a superficial friendship, but rather to a deep relationship with Him. Scripture tells us that not everyone who claims to know Jesus will be acknowledged before the Father by Him. There is a difference in knowing about Jesus, or even preaching and teaching in His name and having a relationship with Him where He will say, "I know you." It is not enough to know who Jesus is, or to even be a "follower" of Jesus. There were plenty of people who followed Jesus around to watch "the show" hoping to see a miracle or be blessed by His presence, but they were not His disciples. We will cover this in more detail in the next chapter, but being a disciple means you are striving to become like the master. This requires a relationship beyond the superficial of just knowing who Jesus is to a deeper level of commitment by surrendering your life to Him.

When we surrender our lives to Jesus, we become a temple for the Holy Spirit as we discussed in Chapter 3. We must embrace the power of the in-dwelling Holy Spirit and recognize that it is through that relationship that we have what Dr. Jim Harris calls in his book by the same name, our *Unfair Advantage*.[32] When the Spirit comes, He brings the spiritual gifts we discussed earlier that we are to use in the fulfillment of our purpose. Since our journey as Paladins is a spiritual one, this relationship is vital to our success to develop into the leaders we are called to be. Without a relationship with the Spirit and letting that power flow through us, we are like a car without an engine. It may look good on the outside. It may even go fast down the hills when being pulled along by gravity, but without the engine it does not have the power to face the challenge of the next uphill climb. Those ups and downs are part of the journey. You need the power of the Holy Spirit to sustain you for the whole journey of developing as a leader and fulfilling your purpose.

Developing this level of relationship with God requires us to constantly be seeking His will for our lives. But how does God reveal His will to us? God reveals His will to us through several communication channels. First, He speaks to us through His written word. All Christian leaders need to allocate time in every day to read and study the Bible. It should be part of your daily stewardship of time that you give back a portion of the day to Him who gave it to you to study His word and listening for what He would have you do each day to advance His Kingdom. Included in that daily allocation of time should be a time for prayer. God speaks to us in prayer through the Holy Spirit that speaks to our hearts. As discussed in Chapter 4, prayer is part of worship where we pursue God to the exclusion of all else. We should be constantly praying bold prayers and expecting extraordinary results when we are in God's will.

Another important aspect of relationship with God is how he speaks to us through other believers. When we are in community with other believers, this is often a way that God confirms other ways He has communicated His will to us. Finally, God reveals His will for our lives through his obvious word that can be found in our circumstances. Whenever someone asks, "How can God let bad things happen to good people?" the assumption is that God is not there with them in the midst of those bad circumstances. If you are in a relationship with God, He is with you always.

 With Others

Jesus also created the model through which we can create deep relationships with others. Jesus developed relationship at various levels even within His own disciples, developing the 12, the three in the inner circle and the one-on-one relationship with Peter. As a leader you may feel like you are being pulled in several directions at once trying to serve the needs of others that you lead. An important distinction in the allocation of your time and effort in the development of others should focus not on "need" but "deserve." Jim Rohn offers in many of his personal development speeches that life does not respond to what you need, but rather to what you deserve.[33] Teach those you lead how to deserve your time and energy in developing them as leaders. Are they dedicated, committed and engaged in the relationship or are they just in it for what they can get out of it? Read about the actions of the disciples in the Book of Acts and you will see that these men were indeed the ones who deserved the time and energy Jesus put into those relationships.

As Christian leaders in the marketplace our relationships with each other need to tend more toward more spiritual over physical, and as noted more transformational over transactional, and covenantal over contractual relationships. Developing relationships allows the leader to leverage the social capital of his or her network of people who are all aligned in their obedience to and relationships with God. This is the basis for trusted relationships within the body of Christ. Leaders who understand the importance of these types of relationships create organizational cultures that foster a climate of collaboration where building a successful team is based on common purpose and mutual respect born out of that trust.

As leaders, our role in developing others is not just about individual connection, but also about helping people to connect and build relationships with others that result in a deeper level of engagement and commitment. Jesus created this type of collaborative environment, noting that the world would know that we are His disciples by how we love one another as the basis for our relationships. This can be challenging at times. We are all flawed people in one way or another, but we do not embrace this calling because it is easy. It is because it is what is required of us as disciples of Christ and what was modeled for us by Jesus in His relationships with others.

As believers we acknowledge that we were built for community, or common unity, and that which we all have in common that unifies us is our belief in and relationship with Jesus. When we fellowship with each other, we strengthen those bonds and allow the Spirit to work in us and through us and our relationships as part of the body of Christ. Do not let busyness get in the way of your relationships. We should like the author of Hebrews 10:25 (NIV) encourages the early church, "Let us not give up meeting together, as some are in the habit of doing, but let us encourage one another…" You are not meant to be on this journey of leadership development alone. Don't fall into the same frame of mind as the prophet Elijah who hid in a cave and thought the Lord had abandoned him and he was all alone. This is the same Elijah who boldly called fire down from heaven in a challenge with the priests of a false god, now doubting himself and God. The Lord revealed in 1 Kings 19: 18 (NIV) that there were 7,000 others in Israel that had never bent their knee to a false god that He had reserved to Himself. Elijah was not alone and neither are you.

The challenge is to be the type of person who inspires others to want to be in relationship with you. From the story of Jonathan, son of Saul, the first king of Israel, we see the type of character that serves as such an inspiration. We can see from the responses of others to him, his armor-bearer, a young David, even the men of Saul's army, that his character is inspirational to them. Even when his own father demands that Jonathan be killed for violating one of his decrees, the soldiers rescued Jonathan from his father and kept him safe. They defied their king because of the relationship they had with Jonathan. You can read more about the faith and character of Jonathan in the leader profile at the end of this chapter.

 ## With Ourselves

In order to have healthy trusting relationships with others, we must have a healthy relationship with ourselves. When we are commanded to love by Jesus in Matthew 22:36-40 (NIV) we are told to love God with all of our heart, soul and mind. Likewise, meaning in the same way, we are to love our neighbors, with the same level of commitment as our love of God, as with ourselves. We cannot love others and we cannot love God, if we hate ourselves. Rather, our self-esteem flows from our confidence of who the Spirit is in each of us.

From Galatians 3:26-29 (NIV) we know that through our faith in Jesus Christ, we are redeemed children of God. We belong to Christ and we are heirs to the promises of God. Also, the Psalmist reminds us (Psalm 139:14, NIV) that as children of God, we are fearfully and wonderfully made. From previous chapters we have discussed that each of us has a divine purpose. Through our trusting relationships with God, others and ourselves we have the faith to trust that God will help us fulfill the purpose for which we were created.

Our relationship with ourselves should not be a narcissistic "look at me" attitude (even though the icon for this section is a person's reflection in a mirror). It should come from the realization that as a redeemed child of God, we have worth and we have value. We cannot effectively lead others to their full potential in a loving relationship with God and others if we do not love ourselves in a positive and healthy way. Jesus modeled this by knowing and acting within His purpose while He was here, yet doing it with gentleness and humility. As leaders it is acceptable to take satisfaction in our work, but we must avoid the temptation of pride.

Peter reminds us in 1 Peter 5:5-7 (NIV) that God sets Himself against the proud, but He shows favor to the humble. This pride can keep us from relying on the relationships we need with God and with others. It can make us think too much of ourselves and that we can complete this journey alone. We are not meant to engage in this struggle alone. Wise leaders admit their need to others in a very transparent way that demands both accountability and allows others to help lift you up in prayer and encouragement. They also rely on God, who cares about them and who will help them through any situation. Being humble allows us to depend both on those in trusted relationships with us and trust our reputation to the Lord and rely on His strength.

Summary

We discussed the importance of love in our relationships with God, others and ourselves. Leaders understand the importance of trusted relationships and invest the time and energy as Jesus did into developing and nurturing those relationships. We acknowledge that our relationships should be more spiritual than physical, transformational over transactional, and covenantal over contractual in nature. We also need to remain humble as we seek to develop the type of character that would inspire others to enter into the depth of relationship that loving God, others and ourselves with all our heart requires.

As you assess yourself against the standards for this discipline, I have divided your relationship with God into the three areas of Father, Son and Holy Spirit so that you can assess your level of relationship with each should you so choose. Although many people are comfortable expressing their relationship with God the Father and with Jesus Christ the Son, my experience is that many of those same people are not as comfortable expressing or having a good understanding of their relationship with the Holy Spirit. Prayerfully consider and let the Spirit guide your answers and to help you focus on ways to improve your scores on your journey of becoming a Paladin.

 ## Self-Assessment

Relationship: The way in which two or more concept, objects or people are connected, or the state of being connected.

Rate yourself on a scale of 1-5 at how well you are being obedient in the areas of relationship discussed in this chapter.

	Not at All=1	Somewhat=2	Frequently=3	Regularly=4	Always=5
God	☐	☐	☐	☐	☐
Jesus	☐	☐	☐	☐	☐
Holy Spirit	☐	☐	☐	☐	☐
Others	☐	☐	☐	☐	☐
Ourselves	☐	☐	☐	☐	☐

Leader Profile – Jonathan: Relationship (1 Sam. 14:7 & 20:17)

The story of Jonathan is one of extreme faith and character and how they impact on our relationships with others. Specifically, we are going to examine Jonathan's relationship with his armor-bearer and with his friend, David.

> *"Jonathan was not focused on personal glory, plagued by indecision, not paralyzed by fear and a lack of faith in the Lord or His timing. "*

It is hard to talk about Jonathan without talking about his father, King Saul. Saul had demonstrated that he was not up to the task of leading Israel well and his actions, whether inspired of greed, fear or pride, caused the Lord to withdraw his favor from him. This had implications for Jonathan as well because it meant that Saul's line would not be a monarchial dynasty. Jonathan, unlike his father, was not focused on personal glory, plagued by indecision, nor paralyzed by fear and a lack of faith in the Lord or His timing. He was also fiercely loyal to his friends.

In Chapter 14, we see the faith and character of Jonathan. The Philistines outnumber the Israelites and have superior weapons and equipment, but this does not deter Jonathan. The chapter starts with, "One day it happened that..." meaning that there was no particular significance to the day. Jonathan just got up and decided to go over to enemy occupied territory with just his armor bearer.

We don't know if Jonathan is just a brash young man, full of himself or if his outrage at the Philistines oppressing his people had reached its limit, or if there was some other motivation. We do know that whatever the reason, Jonathan was the type of leader that inspired his armor bearer to trust in his judgment. In verse 6 he said to his young armor-bearer, "Come. Let's go..." and in verse 7 his young armor-bearer tells him, "Go ahead; I am with you heart and soul." The question for us as leaders is this, "Do we inspire the kind of confidence in those we lead that they are with us heart and soul?"

Jonathan and his armor-bearer boldly attack the Philistine outpost, having first to climb up using hands and feet to get up the cliff and the scripture tells us (verse13) his armor-bearer was right behind him. Once they reach the top, in their first attack,

> *"The question for us as leaders is this, 'Do we inspire the kind of confidence in those we lead that they are with us heart and soul?'"*

Jonathan and his armor-bearer kill about twenty men in an area covering about a half an acre. Jonathan's faith in the Lord, where he acknowledges "Nothing can hinder the Lord from saving, whether by many or by few," and the confidence of his armor-bearer to follow him no matter what he had in mind, set in motion a chain of events whereby the Lord delivered Israel that day.

Next let's examine the relationship that Jonathan had with David as recorded in 1 Samuel Chapter 20. As noted previously King Saul, Jonathan's father was no longer the anointed king of Israel. Which meant that Jonathan was not going to succeed him as the King; David was. However, Jonathan's relationship with David was more important to him that his father's ambition for him or for himself. David has fled from Saul and goes to Jonathan to find out how he has wronged the king that he wants to kill him. At first Jonathan does not believe that his father means David harm, but they devise a plan whereby Jonathan will sound out his father and send David word.

Regardless of the outcome, Jonathan makes a covenant with the house of David and had David reaffirm his oath out of love for him, because he loved him as he loved himself. This is a powerful testimony of the depth of their relationship. This is the same language Jesus uses in Matthew 22:37-39 (NIV) to tell us the greatest commandments, "'Love the Lord your God with all your heart and with all your soul and with all your mind.' This is the first and greatest commandment. And the second is like it: 'Love your neighbor as yourself.'"

Later in verses 24-31 we, and more importantly Jonathan, see Saul's true character when he questions Jonathan about David's whereabouts

DAILY APPLICATION

Follow the example of Jonathan when faced with the challenges of leadership and:

- Model the type of character that inspires others to follow you even in difficult situations

- Be the type of leader that puts the needs of others over your own

- Stand your ground, even in the face of adversity to honor your relationships with others

- Base your relationships on love, not what you can get from the other or some other benefit by being in the relationship

and curses Jonathan for the crime of being David's friend. Saul was so angry that he threw his spear at his own son for honoring his relationship to David over his own interests as Saul's heir to the throne. Jonathan leaves his father's table in anger (not of fear for his life) and ashamed of his father for the way he is treating David, not for just trying to kill him. So deep is his relationship with David, that in spite of his father's actions, he warns David of Saul's intent and in verse 42 tells David to go in peace because they swore friendship with each other in the name of the Lord. As leaders, we should strive to have the depth of friendship that Jonathan inspired in others, regardless of status or station.

When we practice the discipline of relationship, where we love others as we love ourselves, we are demonstrating the character of Jonathan and modeling the type of relationships that show that we are worthy of our walk as Paladins. – the leaders we are intended to be. Follow the steps in the "Daily Application" and you have a blueprint for biblical success.

Chapter 7

Discipleship

"Many think that the price of discipleship is too costly and too burdensome. For some, it involves giving up too much. But the cross is not as heavy as it appears to be. Through obedience, we acquire much greater strength to carry it."

- James E. Faust

Another way to view discipleship is to use the word apprenticeship. A disciple or an apprentice is more than just a follower. They have the express intent to become like the teacher they are following after agreeing to a certain period of apprenticeship where the requisite knowledge, skills and abilities are learned and developed. During this period the apprentice and master work closely together where the master does and the apprentice watches. Then the master allows the apprentice to do while the master watches. Only after a period of development of both skills and trust does the master allow the apprentice to do and then the master follows up after to evaluate how the apprentice has done. As Christian leaders we have to agree to this same level of commitment to be developed by God into the leader we are intended to be. Our challenge is that we cannot see the master's approving nods when we get something right or the slight frown when He sees us perform below our potential. No one ever said following Jesus as a disciple would be easy. Our next avatar struggled with what it means to be a disciple and not just a mere follower of Jesus.

***

Gerard D'Guerin, the "Brave Spear of War." God's Instrument of Spiritual Warfare is our avatar for the discipline of discipleship. Gerard is the oldest of our avatars. His armor, weapons and ways are reminiscent of a previous era. He is sometimes called "the old man" among his peers, but there is still a lot of fight left in him. Gerard has considered himself a follower of Christ for many years and is known as a man of God. However, he felt like something was missing in his life, so he set out on a journey of personal discovery and found the Citadel of Peace. While studying there, his faith grew, and his knowledge of the Lord deepened, but he was still incomplete. His teachers helped him understand that there was more to becoming a disciple of Christ than just following Jesus. They pointed out that throughout His earthly ministry there were plenty of people who followed Jesus for the spectacle of it all. They wanted to see the miracles, hear him teach with authority, see other people changed, but they were never considered His disciples. They failed to respond to Jesus and His message of repentance and redemption.

Gerard argued that he was not like those people because he had responded in faith to the message and accepted Jesus as his Lord and Savior and repented of his sins. They countered with the question, but did you respond in obedience to the command to go and make disciples of all nations, teaching them what he had learned from Jesus? In that moment he knew that he had not. From that moment he started studying what Jesus taught the disciples, not just to deepen his own relationship with Jesus, but also so that he could teach others by sharing the good news of Jesus and become a disciple-maker.

This was when the spiritual attacks against him began in earnest. Gerard realized that he must have been an ineffectual disciple before because he never encountered the spiritual opposition like he did once he started leading others to Christ to make them disciples and disciple-makers. But he lived up to his name and was a brave spear, an instrument of spiritual warfare, that met the enemy head on. When he relied on the power of the Holy Spirit to guide him, the love of God and the body of Christ, his brothers and sisters, to sustain him, he became a great disciple-maker. His teachers had him study the story of Elijah and Elisha as a model for how to mentor an apprentice to be like himself, a disciple-maker. In the process, he mentored other spiritual warriors to join him in his purpose and they became a force to be reckoned with in their community. He and the disciple-makers he was leading started claiming ground from the enemy and advancing the banner of Christ.

Through his time of study and training he learned how to lead others to Christ and how to help them become disciple-makers to lead others to Christ. He began to face each new day with anticipation and committed to look for opportunities to be a disciple-maker. Let's take a look at what Gerard learned on his journey toward becoming a Paladin.

***

Many people claim to be followers of Christ but being a disciple of Christ means more than just following. It means conforming to His image. The first step in the process of becoming like Christ, especially if we are called to lead others forward for Christ, requires our own personal trip to the cross. A personal faith in Jesus as Lord is a prerequisite for Christian leadership. It is the standard by which God assesses us, how well we are doing in our journey of conforming to the image of His Son. When He looks at us, He should see the Lion of

Judah walking courageously in our faith and leading others boldly. We have been given the authority over this world. How well are you doing at exercising the authority given to you by Christ, incorporating discipleship into all aspects of your life and work as you do your part to fulfill the Great Commission from Matthew 28:18-20 (NIV)?

The Great Commission is about more than just the evangelizing task of baptizing but also about the discipleship task of teaching. Jesus commands us to go and teach everything He commanded us. The results of this teaching are life changing requiring responses from us as disciples first. First, it requires a response of faith on our part that we believe that Jesus is everything He told us He was and is. Secondly, it requires a response of obedience to Christ's commands and a continuous devotion to those teachings in every aspect of our lives. In their book, *Your Work Matters to God*, authors Doug Sherman and William Hendricks offer that all that we do should bring honor and glory to God and that in Paul's letter to the Ephesians we are instructed how to do this in five broad categories: in our personal and spiritual lives, in our church life, in our work, in our home and in our communities.[34]

God should be the focal point in every aspect of our lives, not just on Sunday morning. We are called to live a distinctive lifestyle, one we have labeled as that of a Paladin to emphasize that we are engaged in a war. In this war, as all others, the most important thing we can do is obey our orders. Through our response of faith in Jesus as Lord and Master of our lives and though our response of obedience to teach others what we have learned are we able to fulfill our part in the Great Commission. Let's look a little closer at each of these areas.

 ## Response of Faith

God wants to be your partner in all aspects of your life. Do not let your unbelief be an obstacle in your quest to be a better leader. We are children of God through our faith in Jesus Christ. You should trust and believe that He is willing to do miracles in all five areas of our lives as previously mentioned. You should believe that He cares about the outcomes. We must be open to the idea of being discipled by God as we respond in faith to the calling He has for us in all aspects of our lives. This means as Dr. Rick Taylor points out in his book, *The Anatomy of a Disciple*, having a heart that is submitted to the will of the Father, a renewed mind that is biblically transformed, choices that demonstrate who we are at our core and how those choices drive our compassions, and how we relate to the world.[35]

We should respond to that faith, trust that God is who He says He is, and allow ourselves to be discipled by the Holy Spirit. God teaches us His ways and leads us when we are humble. When we are faithful to God, He is faithful and just with us. When we respond in faith by surrendering and committing our lives to Him and His purpose, we are ready to be Jesus' disciple. While displaying this level of commitment as a Christian leader to the Great Commission, where we first respond in faith, we are to trust in and lean on Jesus, as He reminds us at the end of Matthew 28:20 (NIV), "And surely I am with you always, to the very end of the age." While He is with us, He is constantly refining us through the process of becoming more like Him, conforming to the image of Jesus. My personal belief is that this is the standard by which we will be held accountable by God, "How well did you do at conforming to the image of my Son?" With this standard in mind, we grow in our courage and learn to walk worthy of our calling to the life of a Paladin. Being a disciple is not just about following Jesus or doing good works. It is about the process of becoming more like Him by following His example and by boldly doing what He has called us to do.

As a leader you are going to face scary situations. But God has not given you a spirit of fear. From Joshua 1:9 (NIV) the Lord encourages us to not be terrified or discouraged for He will be with us wherever we go. Our courage comes to us when we turn from those scary circumstances toward God and understand that He is stronger than any circumstance we may face. He wants us to rely on His strength to get through those situations and to lean not on our own understanding.

Response of Obedience

Once we have accepted the truth of the good news and respond by faith, we have an obligation to respond in obedience to Christ's commands. We should be ready to respond as Isaiah did in Isaiah 6:8 (NIV) by stating, "Here am I, send me!" As stated earlier this part is a little more difficult for the apprentice whose master is not physically present. However, we are not alone. Jesus said in John 14:12 (NIV), "I tell you the truth, anyone who has faith in me will do what I have been doing. He will do even greater things than these because I am going to the Father." He also promised that once He was gone that the Helper would come in the person of the Holy Spirit who would help us to discern what this obedience should look like.

Like the original converts in the book of Acts, after they responded in faith, they continually devoted themselves to the apostles' teaching, and to obeying those life-changing instructions. For the Paladin, we have a responsibility to devote ourselves to Jesus' life-changing teachings and to passing those commands on to others that we lead. We do this through formal teaching, but we also have to demonstrate that our lives have been changed in how we behave. Since behavior is an outward manifestation of who you are at your core, it will be difficult to convince anyone that you have been changed on the inside, in what you think and feel, if it does not show up in how you act. As we discussed the frieze, the middle section of the entablature of the Citadel of Peace, where our values are demonstrated, what we do is far more important than what we say when we are asking those we lead to accept new behaviors.

As a Paladin, we have to be willing to respond appropriately to how God is moving in our lives, revealing His will for us and for those we are called to lead. When we respond in obedience, with a willing attitude, we are participating in the process of God shaping us. It is through that shaping, that journey of a Paladin, that we fulfill our purpose. This is the great adventure, the epic quest that our lives are meant to be. Anything else is a poor substitution for the life of abundance and meaning that being a disciple of Christ entails. We have a choice to make in our response of obedience. We can face the journey with anticipation of what an adventure it is going to be or with apprehension about how scary it is going to be. Anticipation or apprehension – the choice is yours. Choose anticipation and join God on the adventure He has in store for your life. People want to follow leaders who are going somewhere. There is no greater destination than the port of heaven. Do not lie at anchor. Set sail on the great adventure that you have been called to live and do so boldly so that others may take heart from your example and respond appropriately to the calling on their lives.

 ## The Mantle of Leadership

We started this chapter by equating discipleship to apprenticeship. Before we can mentor another and pass the mantle of leadership, we must first go through the apprenticeship journey ourselves. No matter your station or vocation, everyone should have a mentor who they look to for guidance and support. As I said in the previous chapter, we are built for community. Finding a mentor can be a difficult task, but every leader can benefit from having one. Mentoring is more than just formal training although many leaders have formal arrangements with a coach to satisfy this requirement. Others rely on an informal relationship with an older version of themselves who has blazed a trail through the wilderness they find themselves navigating.

An additional aspect of the mantle of leadership in this mentor-protégé continuum that I want to briefly mention is the inclusion of peers into the equation. Dave Ramsey discusses this in the importance of your role in the "Paul-Barnabas-Timothy model." He notes that as leaders we should pour ourselves into the younger generation and mentor others as Paul mentored Timothy. He also notes how good leaders are willing to be Timothy and sit at the feet of their "Paul" and allow a mentor to pour into them. Really good leaders are those who surround themselves with people who will challenge them and hold them accountable, the "Barnabas" of the equation.[36] By allowing ourselves to be mentored by a peer is a different type of relationship, one that takes a high level of maturity and confidence (and often thicker skin).

These three levels of engagement are at the heart of what it means to wear the mantle of leadership. They are defined by sharing your life with another. This is why finding a mentor can be a difficult task. Each leader should strive to be both mentor and protégé, leading others while being led yourself, while being held accountable by a peer or group of peers. For a leader, mentoring is a way to positively impact the lives of others and to ensure that the multi-generational work of the Lord continues once you are gone. Allowing peers to mentor you is part of that refining process that allows iron to sharpen iron as described in Proverbs 27:17 (NIV). Mentoring others as apprentices or disciples ensures the continuation of God's work as demonstrated in the lives of Elijah and Elisha. More of their story can be found in the leader profile at the end of this chapter.

Summary

In summary, we have examined the final column of the SWORD of Leadership, discipleship, and have examined that how we respond to God, through our faith and our obedience, are important aspects of our discipleship efforts. Have you and do you respond in faith to what God is calling you to do as a leader? Do you demonstrate a willingness to respond in obedience and fulfilling your purpose? Are you doing it with anticipation or with apprehension? When we become a disciple of Jesus, we are more than just followers, we are flowing to learn from Him, observe how He lives and learn to live like Him with the intent to become like Him. Just as the apprentice strives to become like the master, we must strive to become like Jesus. Part of that calling is the process is demonstrating the humility to be discipled by the Spirit and through a mentor who has gone before us as a protégé. Part of that process is allowing a peer (or better a group of peers) to hold us accountable and to challenge wrong behaviors. The final part of this process is being a mentor to someone else so that the multi-generational work of the Kingdom continues after we are gone.

As you assess yourself against the standards for this discipline, assess the level of your responses of faith and obedience in regard to the Great Commission. I have also added the prompt to assess your willingness to be a mentor of another and your willingness to humble yourself to be held accountable by a peer, and as an apprentice or protégé to another leader regarding the mantle of leadership. Prayerfully consider and let the Spirit guide your answers and to focus on ways to improve your scores on your journey of becoming a Paladin.

 **Self-Assessment**

Discipleship: Following a teacher to learn from them, observe how they live and then learn to live like them with the intent of becoming like them.

Rate yourself on a scale of 1-5 at how well you are being obedient in the areas of discipleship discussed in this chapter.

	Not at All=1	Somewhat=2	Frequently=3	Regularly=4	Always=5
Response of Faith	☐	☐	☐	☐	☐
Response of Obedience	☐	☐	☐	☐	☐
Mentor (of Another)	☐	☐	☐	☐	☐
Peer (by Another)	☐	☐	☐	☐	☐
Protégé (to Another)	☐	☐	☐	☐	☐

As an additional area for consideration, if you are interested in a great tool for discipling others, I highly recommend the *Go Book: Foundations* by Joseph Perry.[37] It is a simple yet effective 12-week curriculum to mentor anyone, including new believers, to become disciples and more importantly disciple-makers themselves.

Leader Profile – Elisha: Discipleship (1 Kings & 2 Kings)

To be a disciple means more than just following another. There is a deeper commitment to apprentice oneself to another with the intent of becoming like the master. The discipline of discipleship has two implications for the leader. It means that we must personally model the process of becoming like Jesus, and just as important, to go and disciple others in what it means and how to commit to the process of becoming like Jesus. The discipline of discipleship means to commit to becoming like Jesus and to lead others to do the same. Although the use of the word disciple is mostly found in the New Testament, the concept of following another with the intent of becoming like them is not. One such example is found in the calling and mentoring of Elisha by the prophet Elijah found in both 1 and 2 Kings.

> *"The discipline of discipleship means to commit to becoming like Jesus and to lead others to do the same."*

The story of Elisha begins with his calling as instructed by the Lord in 1 Kings 19:16 (NIV) by Elijah to succeed him as prophet. This is unique in that Elisha was not called directly by God through His reassuring word, visions, dreams or a burning bush, but by Elijah. After his anointing, he is to serve as an apprentice to Elijah for a period of years before finally assuming the duties of prophet over Israel. When he first calls him, Elijah places his mantle or cloak around his shoulders which foreshadows the later passing of the mantle as a symbol of his power and authority as God's prophet to Israel. As leaders, we are called to build up and pour into those that we lead.

When Elijah calls Elisha (1 Kings 19:19-21, NIV), he finds him plowing with twelve yokes of oxen, with Elisha driving the twelfth pair. After Elijah places his cloak around his shoulders Elisha left his oxen and ran after Elijah but asks permission to kiss his father and mother good-bye. Elijah tells him to go back, so he does. He then slaughters his oxen, burned the plowing equipment to cook the meat and then gave it to the people to eat, then he set out to follow Elijah and became his attendant. Elisha demonstrated his commitment to the calling when he slaughtered his oxen, the means of his livelihood, and burned his plowing equipment. He had to examine what claims this call had on him and decide for himself what of his old life he had to leave behind in pursuit of his calling. For Elisha, there was no turning back at this point. He was "all-in."

This also demonstrates Elisha's faith in his mentor and in God's provision. As leaders, do we inspire that kind of faith in our followers that they are "all-in" in their commitment to us, our organization or our mission? As

> *"Leaders must participate in the personal process of growing in spiritual maturity to be like the Lord in character and in conduct."*

noted earlier, part of the discipline of discipleship is first being a disciple yourself. Leaders must participate in the personal process of growing in spiritual maturity to be like the Lord in character and in conduct. People will not want to follow you on this spiritual journey if you do not model the behavior that demonstrates you are also conforming to the image of Christ. Elisha saw what he wanted to be in Elijah. So much so that at the end of their time together, Elisha asked to inherit a double portion of Elijah's spirit.

Just before being taken to heaven in a whirlwind, Elijah repeatedly tells Elisha to stay behind or wait somewhere, but Elisha would not leave him. Do we inspire this kind of loyalty in those that we lead? When Elijah crossed the Jordan with Elisha, just before he was taken to heaven, he rolled his cloak up and struck the water and parted it. As he was taken up to heaven, Elijah dropped his cloak and with it the mantle of leadership and the power and authority of God that it symbolized. Elisha took the cloak and, on his way back, did as Elijah had done, rolling up the cloak, striking the water to part it and crossing back on dry land, signifying that the spirit of Elijah rested now on Elisha.

Are we confident that when we pass the mantle of leadership to someone we are mentoring, that they are capable leaders?

DAILY APPLICATION

From this profile, we see the power of a strong leader who develops even stronger leaders. Elijah mentors Elisha to be an even greater prophet than himself. Exercising the discipline of Discipleship requires:

- Continuing to grow in your own spiritual maturity by exercising the other disciplines to model the character and conduct of Jesus
- Mentoring others to grow in their spiritual maturity
- Commit daily to submit your life to the process
- Encourage those you are mentoring to do the same (even if it means they surpass you)
- Focus on making disciple-makers

A great leader is one that mentors and develops their followers. A Paladin is a leader that embraces the discipline of discipleship and leads himself and others in the spiritual journey toward conforming to the image of Christ.

For the rest of the story, Scripture records that Elijah performed 14 miracles and that it appears that Elisha did inherit a double portion of Elijah's spirit. Scripture further records that Elisha performed 28 miracles, many of which draw striking parallels to the miracles of Jesus such as 20 loaves feeding 100 men, purifying water, and healing people of leprosy.

As a Paladin, embracing the discipline of Discipleship, be like Elijah, mentoring and developing others in their walk of spiritual maturity and conformity toward the image of Christ. Think of the impact you have as a leader should you develop this generation's Elisha, twice as impactful as you have been. To be the leader God intends for you to be requires that you lead diligently and lead not only yourself on your own journey of spiritual growth but lead others in their growth as disciples as well.

Chapter 8

Leadership

"True leadership lies in guiding others to success. In ensuring that everyone is performing at their best, doing the work they are pledged to do and doing it well."

- Bill Owens

We started this journey together with the premise that leadership is a difficult concept to define. My hope is that at this point you have a greater appreciation for what it means to be leader as defined within the Paladin Approach Leader Development System© and by embracing the Citadel of Peace Model at its core, specifically the SWORD of Leadership, you understand what it means to strive to be a Paladin, the leader you are intended to be. But the real question is this: Will you embrace your purpose, pick up the SWORD of Leadership and advance the banner of Christ as a Paladin? It is one thing to recognize that you are in a spiritual fight. It is another thing to actually take your position and stand with your brothers and sisters in Christ and participate in that fight. It is my prayer that you accept this challenge and join us on the battlefield of becoming the leader you are intended to be. It is also my hope that this book has inspired you in some way to do just that.

The remainder of this book is devoted to putting it all together and helping you put together a plan that you can order your life around. Only when you embrace this challenge as a lifestyle change and not just another book about leadership, will you get the full weight of what I am trying to help you accomplish by reading this book. I want to help you create the life infrastructure to handle the God-sized purpose that the Lord has for you and help you use that infrastructure to become the best version of you that you can be within the elements of the model. As with the other chapters we met an avatar that was struggling with some element of the model. Let's meet our final avatar, the leader of the Knights of the Citadel of Peace.

***

Trevelyan DeSerion, whose names mean the one Living in the Citadel of Peace, is the epitome of a Paladin. This is because he has ordered his life around his goal of becoming the leader God intends for him to be. He has come to grips with his beliefs and has declared, in writing, his belief statements regarding each element of the Citadel of Peace and abides there training his mind, body, and soul to be a warrior for Christ. The reason he is our avatar is because in his story we find the guideposts that we need to make the spiritual disciplines of the SWORD of Leadership a part of our daily life as well. However, it is through his struggles and triumphs that we can take heart, especially when we think that we are never going to get there from where we are.

Trevelyan has been a warrior his whole life, starting his training from a very young age. He knew that the life of the Soldier was to be his and he was very proficient with the physical and mental tasks of being a warrior. It was much later in his life that he recognized and began to embrace the spiritual aspects of his calling to the role of leadership and teaching others what it meant to be a Paladin. He, like the other avatars, struggled with each of the elements of the Citadel of Peace, purpose, character, his foundation with Jesus and the SWORD of Leadership that would hold up the God-sized dream that included his purpose.

He began to dwell in the Citadel of Peace and over time began to put the disciplines into practice. He discovered his gifts. He embraced his purpose. He refined his knowledge. He committed himself to the life of a Paladin and ordered his life around his goals of being the best version of himself that he could be. He practiced the discipline of stewardship over everything God had entrusted him with. He practiced the discipline of worship by pursuing God to the exclusion of all else. He practiced the discipline of ownership, accepting responsibility and accountability for his purpose and committing his life to his development as a leader. He practiced the discipline of relationship, connecting with others in the spirit of love so that the world would know he was a disciple of Christ. He practiced the discipline of discipleship, becoming like Jesus and teaching others to do the same.

He now leads the other Paladins in the Citadel of Peace and is actively engaged in the spiritual battle against the enemy, advancing the banner of Christ. He passes his knowledge on to other aspirants on their journey, leading them and teaching them to accelerate their pursuit of excellence and to become Paladins. Let's review one more time the different elements of the Citadel of Peace and what it means to wield the SWORD of Leadership as a Paladin.

***

Citadel of Peace

We started our journey together with an overview of the Citadel of Peace and we reviewed each of the elements of the model and why each is important as we wield the SWORD of Leadership as Paladins. Remember, the Citadel of Peace is a mental model and a spiritual place where you train your mind, body and soul for the rigors of the life of a Paladin. The point of the Citadel of Peace is to hold up your God-sized dreams, which includes your purpose by connecting it to a foundation based on the Lordship of Jesus Christ. The key to ensuring that the columns that represent your disciplines that support that purpose stay in constant and steady contact with your foundation is the entablature of your character, comprised of your vision, values and virtue.

The Citadel of Peace is designed to help you raise your level of awareness as a leader and keep you focused on a few simple disciplines that if repeated every day will make the most difference in your life and as a leader. It is a place to renew your mind and challenge your limiting beliefs that are keeping you from fulfilling your purpose. Remember before you can lead others well, you have to be able to lead yourself well. The model and the material in this book are the underlying concepts and constructs for a system designed to improve yourself as a leader.

Stewardship

To practice the discipline of stewardship often requires a lifestyle change. This starts with your beliefs and attitudes about the elements of stewardship we discussed in Chapter 3. Review your beliefs about each of the five elements of stewardship: time, talent, treasure, temple and testimony when deciding which actions to put into your Paladin Action Plan. Some are more aware of their stewardship of their time and their treasure than they are in the others. Spend time in quiet reflection about how you are stewarding your talents in the service of others, how you are guarding your testimony and how you are taking care of your body as the temple of the in-dwelling Spirit.

 ## Worship

When we worship, we are pursuing God to the exclusion of all else. This should be reflected in our attitude when we pray, praise, and celebrate the victory that is ours in Christ. Remember to incorporate celebrations and thanksgiving into all aspects of each day throughout your week and not just in formal church settings. Pick a few simple disciplines regarding worship and incorporate them into your Paladin Action Plan.

 ## Ownership

When we exercise the discipline of ownership, we embrace this process and complete the action plan as a guide around which we can order our lives. That is the key to this plan. If it is just an academic exercise for you, that once you "get through" the material and complete the plan, you put it on a shelf and never reference it again, it is not going to help you. You must own this and accept that to become a Paladin means that, like an Olympic level athletic with a goal to win gold, you must order your life around these disciplines and your goal to become the leader you are intended to be.

 ## Relationship

To embrace the discipline of relationship, look for ways to deepen your relationship with God through reading His word, prayer and meditation and waiting for His Spirit to speak to you. Join the Lord in a dialogic conversation. Don't just approach Him with a wish list when you need help or are facing adversity. As your relationship with God deepens, so will your relationships with others and yourself. Look for ways to serve others in a spirit of love and strengthen your connections with your brothers and sisters in Christ. Record those actions in your Paladin Action Plan.

 ## Discipleship

Finally, commit to becoming not just a follower of Jesus but a disciple with the intent of becoming like Him. Then examine and record how you are going to participate in the Great Commission while pursuing your purpose, both in your response of faith and your response of obedience. Jesus only has two requirements of us as his followers - to trust Him and to obey Him. When we can do that and teach others to do that, we are not only disciples, but we are developing disciple-makers, doing our part to fulfill the Great Commission.

So now that we know that the columns of the SWORD of Leadership are, what does it mean to wield it. Starting with the firm footing of a solid foundation, and a workable model for internal personal effectiveness, we can use this SWORD to demonstrate how we can adapt to our environment, outside the Citadel of Peace. Just as Jesus modeled the way for His disciples and for us, we can model the example given to us by Christ in our daily interactions with others. Let's take a closer look at what that means in terms of roles, requirements and resources.

 ## Roles

As Christian leaders we are called to be change agents for Christ, by standing on the promises of God and leveraging the power of the Holy

Spirit. As leaders of change have a role to play in ensuring that we are changing the environment we are operating in, not being changed by it, leveraging the opportunities and mitigating the challenges when possible. We are called to be the hero in our own epic tale and not the bit player in someone else's tragedy or comedy. In order to affect change, we must have the trust that comes from living by the SWORD. This begins with our own trust in God that He will be faithful in His promises that are the cornerstone of our relationship with Him. Even though we trust in Him that the battle is already fought and won, our role still requires us (Ephesians 6:11-13, NIV) to put on the full armor of God, to buckle on the belt of truth, don the breastplate of righteousness, stand tall in the shoes of the gospel of peace, affix the shield of faith, wear the helmet of salvation and brandish the sword of the Spirit, and to then stand and take the flaming arrows of the enemy.

 ## Requirements

As Paladins our requirement is to serve others and participate in God's plan. To participate in God's plan is to participate in the ultimate organizational change initiative, the redemption of creation by advancing the banner of Christ. Our internal organizational structure is at its most effective when leaders wield the disciplines of our SWORD in our own lives and practice those disciplines within our organizations. When we accept the requirements of the Great Commission to go, make and teach, we have an action framework for advancing the Kingdom. As with all of our discussions, God levels the requirement on us to participate with Him in everything He has given us to do. Remember He does not call the equipped, He equips those He calls.

 ## Resources

When we engage with God in the diving-human cooperative, everything He has in the way of resources is ours. We just need to have faith and trust in His promises. However, our greatest resources are access to the guidance of the Holy Spirit through the power of prayer and access to the very nature and character of God revealed through His Word. They become the lamp for our feet and the light to our path, the path of a *miles Christianus*, a Christian Soldier and leader – a Paladin.

It is my hope and prayer that after having completed this book you have raised your level of awareness about what it means to be a Paladin and how wielding the SWORD of Leadership is both a challenge and an opportunity. We must stand tall in our purpose and walk worthy of our calling to be the best version of ourselves that we can be; to be the leader we are intended to be.

Conclusion

So, the final question is this. Will you take up the SWORD of Leadership, complete your Paladin Action Plan as you refine your knowledge of God and continue the journey to become a Paladin, the leader you are intended to be? Will you pursue your purpose as a warrior for Christ and advance His banner in all areas of your life? Each Aspirant's Journey is unique, and your Paladin Action Plan will be unique to you as well. The elements discussed in this book make up the core of that plan, but it is up to you to decide to act and what actions you are going to take in relation to your awareness and understanding of each of the elements within the Citadel of Peace and the SWORD of Leadership.

Now that you have finished reading the book, retake the initial assessment and see if your scores have changed as a result of having been exposed to the ideas in this book. I recognize that this is a subjective assessment, as were all the assessments within this book, and their utility will largely be a function of your level of thought and reflection about the various topics discussed. However, some reflection and assessment are better than no reflection and assessment at all.

Final Assessment

I hope that your score will be higher in some areas than in the initial assessment and that I have contributed in some way to your understanding and personal growth in these areas.

Indicate your agreement with the following questions on a 5-point scale with:
1= completely disagree, 2= disagree, 3=neither agree nor disagree, 4= agree, 5= completely agree:

1. I am a disciple of Christ, not just a follower, and as such, I am striving to become more like Christ by submitting to the Lordship of Jesus over my life. ☐

2. I know my God-given purpose in life and how I have been gifted to fulfill that purpose. ☐

3. My character and what I value are consistently reflected in my attitudes and behaviors toward others. ☐

4. I embrace all aspects of the spiritual discipline of stewardship in the service of others because I believe that everything I am and have belong to God. ☐

5. I practice the celebration of worship in all areas of my life, thanking the Lord and demonstrating my gratitude as He blesses me in all areas of my life. ☐

6. I accept the twin disciplines of responsibility and accountability, committing to take ownership of my life, my choices and the consequences with authority. ☐

7. I display the light of Christ in the way that I love others as the standard for all my relationships. ☐

8. I incorporate the responses of trust and obedience required of a disciple into all aspects of my life and work as I do my part to fulfill the Great Commission. ☐

Total Score: ☐

The Paladin's Prayer

My Lord,
I am ready on the threshold of this new day
to go forth armed with your power,
seeking adventure on the high road,
to right wrong,
to overcome evil,
to suffer wounds and
endure pain if need be,
but in all things to serve you
bravely, faithfully, joyfully
that at the end of the day's labor,
kneeling for your blessing,
you may find no blot upon my shield.
Amen.

- Based on an Inscription at Chester Cathedral

The Paladin's Prayer is an adaption to the Knight's Prayer, said to be inscribed on the wall at Chester Cathedral in England. I have included the commentary to provide additional insight into the prayer we pray each day as Paladins.

Review this commentary for a deeper understanding of the prayer and the impact it can have on your life and the lives of others around you.

My Lord, (I acknowledge the sovereignty of God over my life)
I am ready (I have put on the full armor of God and have trained for this day)
on the threshold of this new day (the first thing in the morning, acknowledging each day as a new beginning)
to go forward (not content to sit and wait, but actively engaging with God in the divine-human cooperative, to spread the glory of God throughout all creation in everything that I do)
armed with your power, (with the weapons of God, imbued with the indwelling Holy Spirit, wielding the SWORD of Leadership and possessing the wisdom that comes from pursuing knowledge found in the Word of God)
seeking adventure on the high road, (looking for opportunities to share the gospel to make disciples, while progressing on the narrow way of the path of righteousness as a disciple of Jesus Christ)
to right wrong, (displaying integrity and being a peacemaker)
to overcome evil, (by standing firm against the fiery darts of the evil one)
to suffer wounds (the world will oppose my efforts and try to knock me down. I offer myself as a living sacrifice and I am prepared to suffer for my faith)
and endure pain (the life of a Paladin is not one of ease, but the pain will be worth it. The pain of discipline weighs ounces. The pain of regret weighs tons.)
if need be, (in all things, God's will be done)
but in all things to serve you (as a disciple of Jesus Christ)
bravely, (setting aside my fears and doing what is right)
faithfully, (running the race that has been marked out for me)
joyfully (with a peace that passes all understanding)
that at the end of the day's labor, (when I return to the Citadel of Peace and submit myself to your accountability for what you have entrusted to me)

kneeling for your blessing, (in anticipation of the peace that comes from your grace, regardless of my victories or failures)
you may find no blot (acknowledging that I have made every effort to remain blameless and to be at peace with you, remaining righteous in your sight)
upon my shield. (the measure of faith, given to me by God, in the death and resurrection of my savior - Jesus Christ).
Amen! (so be it).

Use this daily prayer each morning to set your mind on the things of heaven and recognize your role in being not only a disciple, but a disciple-maker. It is a call to start your day in the Citadel of Peace and in the presence of God. Use it to remind you that you are engaged in the spiritual battle to which Paladins are called, to be the best version of yourself that you can be. Look for the opportunities for adventure on the high road and do not shrink from the pain of growth and development as a leader. Our goal is at the end of each day to kneel for God's blessing that we have exchanged the day He gave us for something of value and that we can be found blameless and at peace with God.

What follows is an evening prayer to come back to God and give an account for what you traded for the day you were given. Ask for forgiveness where you missed an opportunity to step up and push back against the darkness. Ask for renewal and peace so that you can rest and be ready to face the next day when you get a new beginning to engage in the spiritual battle into which you have been called. Then you may rest easy knowing the grace and peace of the Lord as you return to the Citadel of Peace and center yourself in alignment with God's will and your purpose.

The Paladin's Evening Prayer

My Lord,
Kneeling for Your blessing at the end of this day,
as I reflect upon my adventures, forgive my
failures, shortcomings and missed opportunities
to push back against the darkness.

Restore my soul and strengthen my spirit
in my pursuit of You.
Repair my armor and sharpen my weapons
as I stand for You.
Renew my resolve, increase my measure of faith
and secure my hope
so that if I am to rise tomorrow to pursue Your
will,
that You may find me then, as now,
worthy of my calling as a child of God.
Amen.

As with the previous prayer, review this commentary and dig deeper into what it means to be a Paladin engaged in doing your part to become the leader that God has called you to be.

My Lord, (Again, as always, I acknowledge Your sovereignty)
Kneeling for your blessing (in anticipation of the peace that comes from Your grace)
at the end of this day, (as I prepare for rest)
as I reflect upon my adventures, (I take the time to offer an account and accept responsibility for how and what I traded for this day)
forgive my failures, (those times I tried to do it by myself and was not up to the task)
shortcomings (those times I completed the task in my own strength and did not get Your desired results)
and missed opportunities (those times I did not even try, whether through fear, ignorance or apathy)
to push back against the darkness. (recognizing the evil exists and it is waiting for the opportunity to rush in like darkness and corrupt everything. The Paladin stands to confront evil and bring the Light of Christ to the world)
Restore my soul (help me to see things from Your perspective with renewed vigor to live for You)
and strengthen my spirit (let the Holy Spirit fill my spirit with power to overcome the weakness of my flesh)
in my pursuit of You. (that Your will be the driving force in my life, not mine)
Repair my armor (smooth out the dents in my righteousness, faith and salvation, tighten the straps on my grasp of the truth and the readiness of the gospel of peace)
and sharpen my weapons (increase my knowledge and understanding of Your word, the power of my prayers and the focus of my worship; help me apply the blood of Jesus to my life and let me boldly proclaim the name of Jesus; and give me the strength to share my testimony)
as I stand for You. (to do my part in the spiritual battles of this life)
Renew my resolve, (remind me of my commitment to You)

increase my measure of faith (so that I may rise and continue my race)
and secure my hope (those things I cannot see but that are promised to me as a child of God)
so that if I am to rise tomorrow to pursue Your will, (if I am given that gift)
that You may find me then, as now, (when You examine my heart)
worthy of my calling (as a *miles Christianus*, a Christian soldier and leader, spreading Your glory throughout all creation)
as a child of God. (heir to the promises as a brother of Christ)
Amen. (so be it!)

My final challenge to you the reader of this book is this – To take up the mantle of leadership and advance the banner of Christ, becoming the leader you are intended to be through the refinement of your understanding of the Citadel of Peace and by actively wielding the SWORD of Leadership. Once again let me remind you that from the passage of Scripture in Matthew 16:18 (NIV) Jesus declares that the Gates of Hell cannot withstand the power and ultimate victory of His church. But that victory includes us joining into the fight by embracing our purpose, especially those of us called to be leaders.

Thank you for letting me be your temporary guide through this part of your journey. Godspeed to you on the rest of your personal development quest to become the leader you are meant to be.

Godspeed!

Paladin Action Plan Template

Complete your personal purpose statement and your personal belief statements regarding the five disciplines of the SWORD of Leadership (If you are unsure of these visit www.swordofleadership.com for more information to assist you).

Included is a sample belief statement that you can adopt or modify. Once you have completed your belief statements, based on your assessments from the book, note those areas that you need to improve, and capture your top three action steps that will make the most difference to you in each of the five disciplines.

As an additional step to prompt you to work on these areas, make a commitment to yourself and sign the Paladin's Pledge both here and at the end of Chapter 2. Refer to these steps and record your progress often.

I, _____, pledge to embrace the life of a Paladin by entering the Citadel of Peace and pursuing the daily disciplines of the SWORD of Leadership to become a warrior for Christ engaged in the spiritual battle to become the leader I am intended to be.

_____
(sign and date)

Godspeed on your journey Paladin. Thank you for letting me be your guide on this portion of it.

My Paladin Action Plan

The call to leadership requires that we as leaders acknowledge biblical truth in each of the disciplines of the SWORD and wield it in service to others. This action plan includes a fundamental belief statement that you must consider.

"I believe that Jesus redeemed leadership when He said, 'Not so with you' and through his example, modeled what it means to lead to serve, not to rule."

Remember the story of Trevelyan DeSerion, and how he embraced the calling of leadership to serve others. As Paladins, we strive to be warriors for Christ and the leaders we are intended to be. This is not an easy life, but it is rewarding. We all want to be like the first two servants from the parable of the talents who hear, "Well done good and faithful servant" and get to share in our master's happiness.

My hope and prayer are that you accept the challenge to become the leader you are intended to be. From Matthew 16:18 (NIV) Jesus declares that the Gates of Hell cannot withstand the power and ultimate victory of His church. The challenge is to stop buying into the current model of Christians behavior, that we must keep playing defense from the walls of our brick and mortar sanctuaries and hope the devil leaves us alone while we are there. The Gates of Hell are in the static position of defense. We are the ones who are supposed to be on offense – taking the fight to the enemy. So, my challenge to you is to take up the SWORD of Leadership, refine your knowledge, skills, attitudes and beliefs, and become a Paladin – the leader you are intended to be.

Use this appendix or a separate journal or notebook, if you prefer, and after prayerful consideration, write down your Paladin Action Plan using the templates for each of the disciplines covered here as a guide.

There are no right or wrong versions of your plan. It is your plan. It should cover those areas that are mentioned in the template and the assessments, especially any that need to be refined or sharpened. You can use the supplied belief statement for each discipline or you can write your own. This is your action plan based on your beliefs.

My Purpose Statement:

"Today I will serve others by _____ _____."

(Work to express your purpose by adding only two action-oriented words to the above sentence.)

Stewardship

The call to stewardship requires that we as leaders acknowledge biblical truth in each of the five areas of stewardship. This action plan includes the following fundamental belief statement that you must consider.

"I believe that all that I have, all that I am responsible for, all that I am, and all that I ever hope to be belong to God."

Remember the story of Joffrey Lévêque, the Guardian of the Citadel of Peace and how he initially struggled with the discipline of stewardship. He was taught to recognize that everything he had was a gift from God and that how he felt in his heart about his stewardship of those gifts was more important than his actions. He learned that stewardship of those gifts meant more than just the mechanical action of giving a portion back to his local church. He found that each of the five T's were integral to his overall effectiveness as a steward and committed to a daily plan of action to remind him of that truth.

Just like with Joffrey, the five T's of this module serve as reference points in our developmental journey and can also be found embedded throughout the story of Nehemiah. The Leadership Profile of Nehemiah is included as a bonus gift with the course. Read it and like Joffrey, follow the example of Nehemiah when daily practicing the discipline of stewardship and:

Seek God's will through prayer

If it all belongs to God, we should constantly be asking Him what He wants us to do with it.

Survey the situation

Assessing the situation in which we find ourselves gives us the opportunity to look at how the stewardship of our time, talent, treasure, temple and testimony could be important to that situation. It allows us to ask the questions to determine if this is the best use of the resources with which we are entrusted. A survey of the situation before committing to any course of action may reveal whether this is something that one should consider supporting or doing, or not.

Recognize that we are created for community and involve others

Although we are called to be stewards of creation, we are not called to do so alone. Nehemiah involved others in his planning and activities. We should too. Consider who else should be involved in your stewardship efforts, whether providing you with "wise counsel" in your decision-making, sharing resources, or leveraging complementary talents and skills.

Recognize that not everyone we involve will want to see us succeed

Not everyone within your sphere of influence will want you to succeed. Unfortunately, there are people, even other Christians, who may feel threatened by your efforts to be good stewards, as if your faithfulness may highlight their perceived unfaithfulness. Abel's own brother, instead of focusing on his own heart and doing what was right, became jealous of him to the point that Cain murdered Abel. We must not let our detractors keep us from being good stewards and making bad decisions to appease them, over doing what is right with what we have been entrusted with by God.

Incorporate biblical best practices into all we do

There is no greater resource or collection of best practices than those found in the Bible. It is primarily a relationship manual that details how we should think, feel and act in our relationship with God and with each other. How we deal with others should be at the core of each of our business practices and the intent and result should always honor God.

Remember to be Spirit-led in pursuit of our calling

We counter the opposition that we are sure to face when we are working within God's will and managing the resources placed in our care to expand God's glory throughout all of creation. The enemy does not concern himself with the 98% who drift through life. They are not a threat to him and his designs. You will be when you join the 2% and actively pursue your purpose and God's will but can withstand the trials that will come when you are Spirit-led in all that you do.

Using this template as a guide, write down your own action plan for how you are going to implement the lessons you have learned from this module about stewardship.

Stewardship: _____

_____
(My personal belief statement regarding stewardship)

Stewardship Action Steps: Date Completed

_____

_____

_____

 Worship

The call to worship requires that we as leaders acknowledge biblical truth in each of the three areas of worship. This action plan includes the following fundamental belief statement that you must consider.

"I believe that God is worthy of praise and thanksgiving for who He is and all that He has done for me."

Remember the story of Nicolas Clarion, Singer of the Song of Victory (that Brings Peace) and how he embraced the discipline of worship. He was taught that worship was more than just singing in the sanctuary. He thought that he had the discipline of worship all figured out because he could sing well and lent his voice to formal services, sharing his gift with others in the sanctuary. He learned that God is worthy of all honor and praise all the time and not just with his voice.

He came to recognize that praise and celebration were not just occasional occurrences but rather these should be our continual state of being because of the victory we enjoy in Christ, even in the face of adversity. When we, like him, follow the example of King Jehoshaphat found in the Leadership Profile for this module, we have an action plan for incorporating the discipline of worship into our daily routine despite those adversities.

Follow the example of King Jehoshaphat when faced with adversity and:

Go to the Lord in Prayer and inquire of the Lord

The Lord is waiting to hear from you in good times and bad. Don't wait until you face adversity to go to the Lord but certainly when it comes, inquire of the Lord how you should proceed.

Humble yourself and admit you do not know what to do, staying focused on the Lord

Keeping your focus on the Lord and His will for your life makes facing adversity easier. We rarely have all the answers, but God does. Don't be afraid to admit you don't have all the answers but know that the Lord will guide you.

Be obedient and lead others in right actions

As a leader, others are watching you and waiting to see how you react to circumstances, both good and bad. If they only see you celebrate in the good times, you are setting a bad example. Be obedient to God, even when it does not make sense and lead others to obedience as well.

Wait for the Spirit

It is sometimes hard to wait for the Spirit, especially in the face of adversity. This is what it means to be Spirit-led. Too often we try to find solutions to problems that God has already solved, or we try to rush God because we think we have the answers. Here is when it is often helpful to employ the wise counsel of others. Some of the clearest messages often come from a word of encouragement or caution from another brother or sister in Christ.

Recognize which battles belong to God and let Him fight them

124

It is often difficult when you are being assaulted from all sides to resist the urge to fight back. Especially when you feel like you can handle the situation. Whether the attacks are spiritual or not, whenever you feel like this remember that you are not called to fight some battles and that ultimately the war has already been won.

Do your part and stand

Even though many of the battles we face are already won by God, this does not exempt us from the requirement to participate. Sometimes the only requirement is to stand. In Ephesians 6 we are constantly reminded that our job is simply to ready ourselves and the stand.

Give thanks to the Lord and worship Him before the battle

As discussed, we must get into the habit of giving thanks in all situations and worshiping God before each of our battles. Before the battle is the hardest time to remember to give thanks and worship God.

Give thanks to the Lord and worship Him after the battle

This is sometimes easier to do which also makes it easy not to do.

Enjoy the abundance of the blessing

Often the blessing is on the other side of the conflict. Remember this when facing adversity.

Know peace

Using this template as a guide, write down your own action plan for how you are going to implement the lessons you have learned from this module about worship.

Worship:

_____

_____

(My personal belief statement regarding worship)

Worship Action Steps: Date
Completed

_____

_____

_____

Ownership

The call to ownership requires that we as leaders acknowledge biblical truth in each of the three areas of ownership. This action plan includes the following fundamental belief statement that you must consider.

"I believe that I am responsible and accountable for everything I do and fail to do with the authority granted to me by God in the pursuit of my calling."

Remember the story of Larissa Navion, Saint of the Citadel of peace and how she embraced the discipline of ownership. She learned that consistency of character and her level of competence were the hallmarks of a leader. She was taught that God desires that she advance His glory throughout all creation and that she had been given a gift to accomplish this, but it must be developed to be used correctly and effectively. She became such an accomplished leader that she came to be admired and venerated because of her character and virtue and became known as the Saint of the Citadel of Peace

Her teachers had her study the leadership of Deborah from the Old Testament and how she had to deal with other leaders like Barak who did not accept the responsibility and accountability demanded of leaders. When we, like her, follow the example of Deborah and Jael found in the Leadership Profile for this module, we have an action plan for incorporating the discipline of ownership into our daily routine. Exercising the discipline of Ownership requires:

Accepting responsibility and accountability

God has a purpose for each of us and when we commit to that ownership assignment, we must accept the responsibility and accountability required of us as children of God for the fulfillment of that purpose.

Recognizing in whose authority you are operating

When God asks us to join Him in His purposes, we are acting within His authority. To do so means that we must submit to that authority and do what is required of us. Whatever the reason, Barak did not recognize that he was operating within God's authority, therefore he was reluctant to follow through without Deborah being involved.

Remembering God has gone before us in everything He asks us to do

When God asks us to step forward in faith and trust Him, He has gone before us and secured the victory for whatever He is asking us to do. This includes not only the accomplishment of your purpose and your calling but even victory over death for those who accept His Son. Take ownership of your calling and step forward boldly.

Taking the lead when God calls

Those with the spiritual gift of leadership must be sensitive to the call to lead and not shy away from that call. God equips those He calls. Our task as leaders is to be Spirit-led, refine our understanding and ability to use those equipping gifts, talents, skills and experiences to take charge of what and who God has called us to lead.

Willingly offering yourself, submitting to God's authority in your life

We, like the children of Israel, are called to boldly advance in our God-given purpose, with the assurance that comes with knowing that we have access to all the authority granted to Jesus by the Father, when we submit our lives to Him. The responsibility and accountability of your calling is less intimidating when you know you have the authority that comes from being called by God to join Him in His purposes.

Recognizing that nothing is impossible for God

When we submit to God's will, exercise the discipline of ownership and take the lead in our calling, we are operating within God's will. When we are operating within God's will, nothing is impossible for the creator of the universe.

Using this template as a guide, write down your own action plan for how you are going to implement the lessons you have learned from this module about ownership.

Ownership:

_____

_____

(My personal belief statement regarding ownership)

Ownership Action Steps: Date Completed

_____

_____

_____

 Relationship

The call to relationship requires that we as leaders acknowledge biblical truth in each of the three areas of relationship. This action plan includes the following fundamental belief statement that you must consider.

"I believe that without love there can be no relationship and that loving God, others and myself is the root of all healthy relationships."

Remember the story of Aram Kassar, and how he embraced the discipline of relationship. He was taught not to focus on his differences with others, but rather what unified them – the love of Jesus. His teachers taught him and showed him the love of God as the basis for all relationships. They taught him that to be the leader others would follow meant that he had to foster the type of relationships that were centered on God and His love.

His teachers stressed that the life of a Paladin was not one of solitude or loneliness. As part of the body of Christ, we all have a part to play. We are designed out of community and for community and that how we love others reflects how we love God. His teachers taught him the lessons of leadership from the story of Jonathan from the Old Testament and showed him how to be a leader like Jonathan that relied on God and inspired others to follow

Through his time of study and training he learned how to love God, others and himself in such a way that his relationships became an example for others to follow. Like Aram, when we follow the example of Jonathan found in the Leader Profile for this module, we have an action plan for incorporating the discipline of relationship into our daily routine. Follow the example of Jonathan when faced with the challenges of leadership and:

Model the type of character that inspires others to follow you even in difficult situations

When we are consistent in our character and conduct, those who follow us know what to expect and we tend to behave in ways that calm and reassure others when things are difficult. Knowing we are children of God and called to His purpose gives us a standard for our character and conduct. We should emulate the character and conduct of Christ in all situations so that when we say to those we lead, "Come let's go," they will follow with all their heart and soul.

Be the type of leader that puts the needs of others over your own

There is a common saying in the US military, "Leaders eat last." This reflects a leadership philosophy that puts the needs of the Soldiers ahead of the needs of the leader. Jonathan modeled this kind of leadership when he put his friendship with David ahead of his own father's ambitions for him as his royal heir. When we lead to serve rather than to rule, we are more in touch with the needs of those we lead.

Stand your ground, even in the face of adversity to honor your relationships with others

How many of us are willing to stand up for what is right, regardless of the personal cost to ourselves? Here is where the courage of your convictions is on display, when you have something to lose. Jonathan knew that supporting his friend David meant that he would never be the king. He also stood up for what was right even though it angered his father Saul, to the point that he threw a spear at his son. He should strive to be like Johnathan who honored the covenant commitment he made to David no matter the cost.

Base your relationships on love, not what you can get from the other person or some other benefit by being in the relationship

Having any type of relationship that is built on anything other than love is not strong enough to withstand the pressures of life, especially for a leader. Don't base your relationships on what you can get from it whether physical or intrinsic. The basis for your relationships with others should be your love of the Father, your love for them and your love for yourself. Any benefits to you should only be ancillary to the relationship and not the point of it.

Relationship:

_____

_____

(My personal belief statement regarding relationship)

Relationship Action Steps: Date Completed

_____

_____

_____

 Discipleship

The call to make disciples of all nations requires that we as leaders acknowledge biblical truth in each of the areas of discipleship. This action plan includes the following belief statement that you must consider.

"I believe that to be the leader you are intended to be requires you to go and lead others to the good news of Jesus Christ."

Remember the story of Gerard D'Guerin, Instrument of Spiritual Warfare (so that you may know peace) and how he embraced the discipline of discipleship. He learned that being a follower of Jesus was not enough. He had to become a disciple, one who seeks to become like his teacher. More importantly, he learned that it meant being a disciple-maker, responding not only to the call of faith, but also the call of obedience to go and make disciples, teaching them what Jesus taught us.

He also discovered that the enemy was not happy when he started taking ground and started to oppose him more. He relied on the guidance of the Holy Spirit, the love of God and the body of Christ, his brothers and sisters, to sustain him through that fight and he lived up to his name as an Instrument of Spiritual Warfare. He learned from the example of Elijah and Elisha from the Leadership Profile that accompanies this module. From this profile, we see the power of a strong leader who develops even stronger leaders. Elijah mentors Elisha to be an even greater prophet than himself. Exercising the discipline of Discipleship requires:

Continuing to grow in your own spiritual maturity by exercising the other disciplines to model the character and conduct of Jesus

To lead others to Christ, you must first know Him, not just know about Him. This deepening relationship is the path to spiritual maturity and the practice of all the spiritual disciplines of the SWORD of Leadership.

Mentoring others to grow in their spiritual maturity

It is still not enough just to know Christ, we must endeavor to become like Him which means we mentor others to become disciples and disciple-makers as well. Teaching and mentoring others to be disciples of Jesus and disciple-makers for Jesus is how you and the one being mentored grow in spiritual maturity.

Committing daily to submit your life to the process

Each day is a new beginning, a new adventure and an opportunity to start fresh in our efforts to practice the discipline of discipleship. But because it is a new day, it takes a new, fresh commitment to submit your will to the will of God and be about your Father's business just as Jesus was when He was creating disciples to further the Kingdom.

Encouraging those you are mentoring to do the same (even if it means they surpass you)

By setting the example for those you are mentoring, it makes it easier for them to do the same. Your encouragement to them will mean less if they do not see you doing what you are asking them to do. Also, you should encourage those you are mentoring to grow as much as they can in their faith and spiritual maturity, even if it means surpassing you in the process. Every leader should desire that those they lead outgrow them, especially in spiritual maturity and the discipline of discipleship, in their efforts to make new disciples and disciple-makers.

Focus on making disciple-makers

In your discipleship efforts, make sure that you are not leading people to be your disciples, but that you are leading them to become like Jesus. Strive to be like the Apostle Paul that told his followers to follow him, not to be like him, but to be like Christ. In those efforts make sure your focus is on making disciple-makers. It is not enough to be like Gerard before he came to the Citadel of Peace and think that the response of faith is enough. That is only half the requirement. The response of obedience to go and make disciples is also required of those of us who follow Jesus.

As you grow in your spiritual maturity within the discipline of discipleship, expect the attacks of the enemy to increase. You will no longer be in the 98% of the people who drift through life. You will be in the 2% making a difference and that will draw the attention of the evil one. As a Paladin, your training in the Citadel of Peace, learning to wield the SWORD of Leadership, will prepare you for those attacks.

This discipline is the most important of the five and is the one that connects all the others together, back through your purpose, to what it means to be a Paladin. Everything you do as a Paladin should have an element of the Great Commission somewhere in it. Use what you have learned in this book to grow and develop as a Christian leader and live the lifestyle of a Paladin.

Discipleship:

_____

_____

(My personal belief statement regarding discipleship)

Discipleship Action Steps: Date Completed

_____

_____

_____

Once you have completed your Paladin Action Plan, refer to it often as you contemplate and assess your growth as a leader. Once you master the top three, revisit the daily application steps for each discipline and see where you need to focus your energies and what limiting beliefs you may still have regarding that discipline and its impact on your continued development as a leader. The journey of a Paladin, the quest to be the leader you are intended to be, never ends. Onward *miles Christianus;* onward warrior for Christ!

If you have found this information helpful and wish to learn more about personal or group coaching using the Paladin Approach, visit www.strategicinfluencealternatives.com and book a discovery call.

If you would like to book Dr. Owens to speak about the SWORD of Leadership contact us at info@swordofleadership.com for his availability.

Endnotes

Chapter 1

1. Paladin. (2019). In *Dictionary.com.* Based on the Unabridged Random House Dictionary. Retrieved from https://www.dictionary.com/browse/paladin

2. Bulfinch, T. (1913). *The age of fable.* New York: Review of Reviews. Published April 200 by Bartleby.com www.bartleby.com/bulfinch/; © 2000 Copyright Bartleby.com, Inc.

3. Eldredge, J. (2001). *Epic: The story God is telling.* Nashville, TN: Thomas Nelson.

4. From the Italian *Chi Cerca Trova,* meaning he who seeks finds. Retrieved from https://mymemory.translated.net/en/Italian/English/chi-cerca-trova

5. Nec Temere Nec Timide. (2019). In *Glosbe.com.* Retrieved from https://glosbe.com/la/en/nec%20temere%20nec%20timide

6. Incepto Ne Desistam. (2019). In *Globse.com.* Retrieved from https://glosbe.com/la/en/Incepto%20Ne%20Desistam

7. Praesis Ut Prosis, Ne Ut Impresse. (2019). In *Globse.com.* Retrieved from https://glosbe.com/la/en/praesis%20ut%20prosis%20ne%20ut%20imperes

Chapter 2

8. Citadel. (2019). In *Dictionary.com.* Based on the Unabridged Random House Dictionary. Retrieved from https://www.dictionary.com/browse/citadel

9. Peace. (2019). In *Dictionary.com.* Based on the Unabridged Random House Dictionary. Retrieved from https://www.dictionary.com/browse/peace

10. Copyright © 2005 Dorena DellaVecchio, Ph.D. Retrieved from www.gifttest.org

11. Welchel, H. (2018). Do you know the purpose of your gifts and talents? [Article]. *The Institute for Faith Work & Economics.* Retrieved from https://tifwe.org/the-purpose-gifts-and-talents/

12. Virtue. (2019). In *Merriam-Webster.com.* Retrieved from https://www.merriam-webster.com/dictionary/virtue

13. Hill, N. (2011). *Outwitting the devil: The secret to freedom and success.* New York, NY: Sterling Publishing.

14. Holmes, O. W. (n.d.). Oliver Wendall Holmes, Sr. quotes in *Goodreads.com.* Retrieved from https://www.goodreads.com/author/quotes/1203736.Oliver_Wendell_Holmes_Sr_

15. Sanders, J. O. (2007). *Spiritual leadership: A commitment to excellence for every believer.* Chicago, IL: Moody Publishers.

Chapter 3

16. Taylor, R. (2013). *The anatomy of a disciple: So many believers, so few disciples.* Fresno, CA: The Well Community Church.

17. Sanders, J. O. (2007). *Spiritual leadership: A commitment to excellence for every believer.* Chicago, IL: Moody Publishers.

18. Senge, P. (2006). *The fifth discipline: The art and practice of the learning organization* (Revised and Updated). New York, NY: Crown Publishing.

19. Eldred, K. (2010). *The integrated life: Experience the powerful advantage of integrating your faith and work.* Montrose, CO: Manna Ventures, LLC.

20. Ashes Remain (2011) On my own. On *What I've Become* [CD] Brentwood, TN: Fair Trade Services.

Chapter 4

21. Worship. (2019). In *Dictionary.com.* Based on the Unabridged Random House Dictionary. Retrieved from https://www.dictionary.com/browse/worship

22. Emerson, R. (n.d.) Ralph Waldo Emerson quotes in *Goodreads.com.* Retrieved from https://www.goodreads.com/author/quotes/12080.Ralph_Waldo_E merson

23. Gills, J. (2003). *The prayerful spirit: Passion for God, compassion for people.* Lake Mary, FL: Creation House.

24. Acuff, J. (2017). *Finish: Give yourself the gift of done.* New York, NY: Portfolio/Penguin.

25. West III, F. (2016). *God's business: How to supercharge your faith, your profit and your client experience.* New York, NY: Morgan James Publishing.

26. Klausmeier, M. (2016). *Corporation reformation: Aligning your life and life's work with the present and future Kingdom.* Xulon Press.

Chapter 5

27. Marshall, T. (2003). *Understanding leadership.* Grand Rapids, MI: Baker Books.

28. Klausmeier, M. (2016). *Corporation reformation: Aligning your life and life's work with the present and future Kingdom.* Xulon Press.

Chapter 6

29. Relationship. (2019). In *Dictionary.com.* Based on the Unabridged Random House Dictionary. Retrieved from https://www.dictionary.com/browse/relationship

30. DePree, M. (1989). *Leadership is an art.* New York, NY: Dell Publishing.

31. Phillips, J. (1987). *Bible explorer's guide: How to understand and interpret the Bible.* Grand Rapids, MI: Kregel Publications.

32. Harris, J. (2015). *Our unfair advantage: Unleash the power of the Holy Spirit in your business.* Houston, TX: High Bridge Books.

33. Rohn, J. (2010). *The treasury of quotes by Jim Rohn: America's foremost business philosopher.* Lake Dallas, TX: Success Books.

Chapter 7

34. Sherman, D. & Hendricks, W. (1987). *Your work matters to God.* Colorado Springs, CO: Navpress.

35. Taylor, R. (2013). *The anatomy of a disciple: So many believers, so few disciples.* Fresno, CA: The Well Community Church.

36. Ramsey, D. (2015). Everyone needs a Paul, a Timothy and a Barnabas [Web log post]. Retrieved from https://www.stewardshipcentral.org/posts/everyone-needs-a-paul-a-timothy-and-a-barnabas

37. Perry, J. (2018). *The go book: Foundations.* Published by the author.

About the Author

Dr. Thom Owens is the lead trainer and principal strategist at Strategic Influence Alternatives, LLC, a leader development organization focused on developing deliberate, purposeful leaders to a higher standard of excellence for greater impact. He retired from the U.S. Army as a Lieutenant Colonel after 20 years of service in combat arms and special operations assignments. Since leaving the service, he has served in executive positions in both for profit and not-for profit organizations over the last 10 years. He has earned his Doctor of Strategic Leadership from Regent University and currently serves as adjunct faculty teaching business and leadership in the College of Arts and Sciences at Regent University.

He also serves as the President of the Christian Business Coalition of Hampton Roads, a tax-exempt business league that exists to develop Christian leaders to fulfill their purpose through business.

He has been married to his wife Tonya for over 30 years and they have four daughters.

Made in the USA
Columbia, SC
15 February 2019